Oct '96

Greg = $\vec{\nabla}$
This
Happy Something!
"Dazed + Confused"
4 →

♡,
Heather
Vogel

Marilyn Werden
and
David Arenson

A Fireside Book
Published by Simon & Schuster
New York London Toronto Sydney Tokyo Singapore

F

FIRESIDE
Rockefeller Center
1230 Avenue of the Americas
New York, New York 10020

FIRESIDE and colophon are registered trademarks
of Simon & Schuster Inc.

Designed by Hyun Joo Kim

Manufactured in the United States of America

1 3 5 7 9 10 8 6 4 2

Library of Congress Cataloging-in-Publication Data
Werden, Marilyn.
Disco Nixon/Marilyn Werden and David Arenson.
p. cm.
"A Fireside book."
1. United States—History—1969–   —Miscellanea.   I. Arenson,
David.   II. Title.
E839.W47   1995   94–36119
973.924—dc20   CIP

ISBN: 0-671-89816-7

To David, my *sine qua non*.

—M.

To Marilyn, the best thing about the ′70s and all the

decades of my life.

—D.

CONTENTS

8 * *Contents* *

9 * *Contents* *

WHY THE '70S LIGHT UP OUR LIVES

When the 1970s ended, a lot of people were glad to see them go. After all, who had fond memories of Pet Rocks or Patty Hearst or plaid leisure suits?

But recently, in one of pop culture's periodic twists of fate, the '70s have come back. First Nixon was, in theory at least, rehabilitated. Then the Coneheads made a movie. Now disco is becoming popular again. What's next? A Southern Democrat in the White House? An Eagles reunion?

Why on earth is this happening? What could possibly have occurred to make the once-scorned '70s look better and better, to the point where Greg from *The Brady Bunch* is running around giving lectures on college campuses?

One clue may be found in the words of ex-Partridge David Cassidy, who said not long ago while planning a concert tour celebrating the '70s, "It was the last decade dedicated to having a good time."

Or, as the owner of L.A.'s Club 1970 recently pointed out, "Everyone has nostalgia for their childhood, their adolescence, or their college days. Now it's another generation's turn."

Yes, the kids who thought Kiss looked cool in that Tammy Faye–kabuki makeup are now starting to experience receding gums and receding hairlines. They are raising families and running corporations. Some of them may even be in the White House assisting in the formulation of domestic and foreign policy, which is kind of scary when you stop to think about it.

If you graduated from high school or college during the '70s, you probably remember Betty Ford before she was a clinic and Ayds when it was a diet candy. You had no way of knowing then that "Truckin'" and "Hot Blooded" would end up as elevator music or that Gopher would get elected to Congress. You were young and innocent and quite possibly stoned much of the time, and it never occurred to you that what you were living through would one day be considered the good old days.

But America's renewed fascination with the decade that brought us Pong, Love Canal, and the AMC Gremlin is not limited only to those whose formative years were twisted by it. Many young people today have caught, shall we say, boogie fever. They are wearing choker collars and flared pants and loud shirts. Keep in mind the David Cassidy fun-decade theory. They are latching onto that good-times-'70s-laid-back-touchy-feely thing, which contrasts so favorably with mean-spirited '90s stuff like drive-by shootings and Rush Limbaugh.

All this explains why you can't turn around nowadays without bumping into another article on the return of '70s chic, or commercials for '70s music, or full-page ads for—have we lost our senses *again?*—'70s fashions.

It also means that the time has come, at last, for *Disco Nixon*. We could have called it *Heavy Metal Carter*, but when you think of the '70s, Nixon and disco come to mind first. The decade's political spasms can be attributed almost entirely to Nixon, without whom there would have been no Ford and probably no Carter (and no threat of a President Agnew, to which we came perilously close). And disco, well, nothing quite says "1970s" like tight pants, big hair, incessant thumping, and song lyrics that start with "Freak out!"

Yes, that's the way, uh-huh, uh-huh, we liked it. And now, through the challenge of a thousand or so trivia questions, all America can relive the glory days of Watergate, thrill again to the Village People, and once more laugh at the zany antics of Sandy Duncan and Idi Amin.

As you turn these pages, may the force be with you.

'70s 1-A

There are certain things that anyone who lived through the '70s ought to know. How lucky we are not to have to do it again, for example. Still, the decade exuded a certain charm, like a bad movie that manages to be entertaining in spite of itself. The production values were clunky, the costumes garish, the script uneven, and the actors oddly out of place, but there was something mesmerizing about it. We couldn't wait to see what unimaginably strange thing would happen next.

Here are ten questions to get you started. Have a nice day.

1. Who said, "I am not a crook"?
2. Speaking of which, what did CREEP stand for?
3. What planet were the Coneheads from?
4. And where did they say they were from?
5. What was "the moral equivalent of war"?
6. Who was Tony Manero?
7. Who won the Battle of the Sexes, in tennis at least?
8. What's the proper response to the question "Are we not men?"
9. Quick! Who was Gerald Ford's vice president?
10. And just who did coin the phrase "The Me Decade"?

(answers on page 173)

People 1

1. What did newspaper heiress Patty Hearst list as her occupation when she was booked into jail after her arrest by the FBI in 1975?
2. Who were Allison Krause, Jeffrey Miller, Sandra Lee Scheuer, and William K. Schroeder?
3. After *Hustler* publisher Larry Flynt had been shot and paralyzed, who counseled him to become a born-again Christian?
4. Following his conversion, Flynt changed *Hustler*'s highly controversial comic, "Chester the Molester"—about a man who preyed on young girls—to "Chester the _____." What?

5. "An odd man . . . unpleasant . . . very artificial . . . I never understood how he became a politician. He really dislikes people." Who described Richard Nixon with these words when he thought the mikes were off at a black-tie dinner?

6. What did Stevie Wonder blame, at least partially, for the 1974 breakup of his marriage to Syreeta Wright?

7. Despite pleas from organizations opposed to the death penalty, this Utah murderer actually wanted to be executed. On January 17, 1977, he was killed by a firing squad in the first U.S. execution in 10 years. Name him.

8. What did Maria Rubio of New Mexico find on her tortilla in 1978 that attracted thousands of pilgrims to her home?

9. Name the political wife who stayed up all night partying with the Rolling Stones at Toronto's El Mocambo nightclub and then at the group's hotel suite, even though it was her sixth wedding anniversary.

10. Just before Super Bowl X, who said of Dallas Cowboys quarterback Roger Staubach, "I hope a shark bites his arm off"?

11. Whose body was stolen in 1978?

12. What politician called California "the meeting place of the inner and the outer universe"?

13. How did Japanese soldier Shoichi Yokoi spend the 28 years from the end of World War II until 1972?

14. Shirley Temple Black became a U.S. ambassador in 1974. To where?

15. In 1978 David and Julie Nixon Eisenhower had a daughter. What was their baby's name?

(answers on page 173)

True or False? 1

Eight of the following 10 items are true. Can you ferret out the two fakes?

1. Chewbacca the Wookie had his own TV Christmas special in 1977.

2. Pope John Paul II recorded an album of original folk songs and in 1979 joined ASCAP so that he could collect royalties.

3. In 1973 the American Bar Association proposed the removal of criminal

penalties against possession and casual distribution of marijuana.
4. The Soviet space station Salyut 6 was plagued by houseflies.
5. In 1979 a man named Robert Edward Lee legally changed his name to Roberto Eduardo Leon so that, as a Spanish-surnamed individual, he would become entitled to preferential hiring and promotion practices under federal affirmative-action laws.
6. Besides books by defendants, unindicted co-conspirators, and the like, the Watergate scandal also spawned a children's book, a cookbook, and a porno book.
7. There was once a seventh member of the Village People who dressed as a bullfighter.
8. New Jersey college professor Edwin Avril set his federal tax return to the music of a Bach cantata in 1977, and on April 16 of that year a 60-voice choir performed the work, which concluded with the stirring chorus "rebate."
9. At Patty Hearst's 1979 wedding, the maid of honor was the daughter of the owner of the bank that Hearst had robbed in 1974.
10. Amy Carter was heard to complain loudly when it was suggested that she attend the 1978 White House Halloween party dressed as a peanut "again."

(answers on page 173)

TV 1

1. Name the five women who played *Charlie's Angels* during the '70s.
2. OK, now, name the *characters* they played.
3. Who was the Fernwood Flasher?
4. What did Archie Bunker call "WASP soul food"?
5. Who published *The Blue Ridge Chronicle?*
6. Producer Lorne Michaels appeared on *Saturday Night Live* in April 1976 and appealed to the Beatles to reunite on the *SNL* stage. How much money did he offer them to appear?
7. What was Potsie's real name on *Happy Days?*
8. How do you say good-bye in Orkan?

Give the names of the four largest mammals in this picture. *(Photo credit: Gerald Ford Library)*

9. Former Georgia Governor Lester Maddox walked off the set of this talk show when its host challenged his segregationist views. Name the show.
10. What did Lieutenant Dan "Hondo" Harrelson command?
11. Who was Phoebe Figalilly?
12. Former real-life New York policeman Eddie Egan played watch commander Bernie Vincent on what TV program?
13. Although it got respectable ratings, *Bridget Loves Bernie* was cancelled after just one season. Why?
14. What was the name of the grizzly bear on *The Life and Times of Grizzly Adams?*
15. The PBS show *An American Family* was a cinema verité portrait of a family in which the nation got to watch as the parents divorced and the eldest son declared his homosexuality. What was the name of the family?

(answers on page 174)

Songs 1

Below are the first lines of some '70s songs. Give the names of the songs and the people who performed them. We'll start off with a couple of easy ones.

1. "There's a lady who's sure all that glitters is gold and she's buying a . . ."
2. "Did you write the book of love and do you have faith in God above?"
3. "Freak out!"
4. "He was born in the summer of his twenty-seventh year."
5. "I couldn't stop moving when it first took hold."
6. "Mama pijama rolled out of bed and she ran to the police station."
7. "Madman drummers bummers and Indians in the summer with a teenage diplomat."
8. "Now, I've been happy lately."
9. "If I could stick my pen in my heart."
10. "Talkin' to myself and feelin' old."
11. "Sometimes in our lives, we all have pain, we all have sorrow."
12. "So I'd like to know where you got the notion."

13. "Well, the southside of Chicago is the baddest part of town."
14. "Where can you find pleasure, search the world for treasure, learn science and technology?"
15. "Nibblin' on sponge cake, watchin' the sun bake."

(answers on page 174)

Women 1

1. Name the attorney who successfully argued *Roe v. Wade*, the case that gave women the right to abortion during the first trimester, before the U.S. Supreme Court.
2. After the Supreme Court ruled most laws prohibiting abortion unconstitutional in *Roe v. Wade*, how many states had laws that were struck down?
3. Why was Francine Hughes able to "get away with murder"?
4. According to Las Vegas bookmakers, what were the odds in the Battle of the Sexes?
5. Why did the state of Missouri sue the National Organization for Women in 1978?
6. In 1973 singer Judy Collins, with Jill Godmilow, made the documentary *Antonia: A Portrait of a Woman*. Nominated for an Academy Award, it depicted this conductor's decades-long struggle against sexism in the symphonic community. Name the conductor (who, incidentally, was Collins' former piano teacher).
7. What was New York's WABC-TV weatherman Tex Antoine referring to when he said on-camera in 1976, "Confucius once say, 'If rape is inevitable, lie back and enjoy it'"?
8. What was "Take Back the Night"?
9. Why did more than 100 women occupy the offices of *Ladies' Home Journal* in 1970?
10. What year was designated International Women's Year by the United Nations?
11. Why, in 1975, did members of the New York Rangers petition to bar women reporters from the players' locker room?
12. Who was elected the first woman mayor of Chicago?

13. In 1972 the University of Minnesota let women do something for the first time. What?

14. Which of the following items did Women for the Free Future burn during a demonstration in Berkeley, California, in 1970?

> Barbie doll
> Bra
> Bible
> Diploma
> Birth control pills
> Book by Norman Mailer
> *Good Housekeeping's* list of the Ten Most Admired Women

15. What financial institution did writer Betty Friedan, designer Pauline Trigere, and New York City Councilwoman Carol Greitzer, along with 12 others, start in New York in 1975?

(answers on page 175)

News 1

1. What highly touted but barely visible comet passed by Earth in early 1974?

2. Who was put to work sorting mail when U.S. Post Office workers went on strike in 1970?

3. What made Arthur Bremer famous?

4. Why was Ford Motor Company indicted for murder in 1978?

5. What was the deadly potion drunk by the followers of the Reverend Jim Jones?

6. According to the chairman of Consolidated Edison, what caused the 1977 New York City blackout?

7. What happened to the U.S.S. *Liberty*?

8. Who was Field Marshall Cinque?

9. What did the people of George, Washington, do for the Bicentennial?

10. Who made *nolo contendere* a household phrase, at least for a month or two?

11. What militant Native American organization held 11 people hostage for 71 days in Wounded Knee, South Dakota, in 1973?

12. Name the head of the Office of Management and Budget who resigned in

1977 amid investigations into his banking practices.

13. In 1972 what did the U.S. Supreme Court decide was "cruel and unusual punishment"?

14. "Theoretically what happened could not happen," said a U.S. Bureau of Reclamation official after this new dam on Idaho's Snake River burst in 1976, killing 11 people and washing away 4,000 homes. What was the name of the dam, which engineers had been warned not to build because of the area's porous rock and soil?

15. In 1974 the sale of something became legal in the U.S. for the first time since 1933. What?

(answers on page 176)

Quotes 1

Who said:

1. "I hear that whenever anyone in the White House tells a lie, Nixon gets a royalty."

    a. Dick Cavett
    b. Johnny Carson
    c. John Dean
    d. Richard Nixon

2. "There are only so many lies you can take, and now there has been one too many. Nixon should get his ass out of the White House—today!"

    a. Sam Ervin
    b. Edward Kennedy
    c. Martha Mitchell
    d. Barry Goldwater

3. "The longer I am out of office, the more infallible I appear to myself."

    a. Richard Nixon
    b. Eugene McCarthy
    c. Henry Kissinger
    d. Earl Butz

4. "Anybody that wants the presidency so much that he'll spend two years organizing and campaigning for it is not to be trusted with the office."

    a. *David Broder*
    b. *David Brinkley*
    c. *Walter Mondale*
    d. *Billy Carter*

5. "Power is the ultimate aphrodisiac."

    a. *Pierre Trudeau*
    b. *Henry Kissinger*
    c. *Idi Amin*
    d. *Jim Jones*

6. "They've asked me everything but how often I sleep with my husband. And if they'd asked me that, I would have told them, 'As often as possible.'"

    a. *Farrah Fawcett-Majors*
    b. *Bo Derek*
    c. *Martha Mitchell*
    d. *Betty Ford*

7. "Falling madly in love with someone is not necessarily the starting point to getting married."

    a. *Hugh Hefner*
    b. *Elizabeth Taylor*
    c. *Sun Myung Moon*
    d. *Prince Charles*

8. "We are moving towards a world not merely of throwaway products but throwaway friends and marriages."

    a. *Marshall McLuhan*
    b. *Alvin Toffler*
    c. *Margaret Mead*
    d. *Maharishi Mahesh Yogi*

9. "Marriage is a great institution, but I'm not ready for an institution yet."

    a. *Woody Allen*
    b. *Warren Beatty*
    c. *Tom Jones*
    d. *Mae West*

10. "I feel like I'm married to this guy named Art. I'm responsible to my Art above all else."

   a. Joni Mitchell
   b. Judy Chicago
   c. Yoko Ono
   d. Liberace

11. "I have sacrificed everything in my life that I consider precious in order to advance the political career of my husband."

   a. Muriel Humphrey
   b. Eleanor McGovern
   c. Pat Nixon
   d. Martha Mitchell

12. "I can't be a rose in any man's lapel."

   a. Margaret Thatcher
   b. Margaret Trudeau
   c. Bette Midler
   d. Quentin Crisp

13. "It is becoming more generally recognized that the home is not the only place for women."

   a. Pat Nixon
   b. Judy Agnew
   c. Queen Elizabeth II
   d. Elizabeth Ray

14. "When Hugh Hefner comes out here with a cottontail attached to his rear end, then we'll have equality."

   a. Jane Pauley
   b. Florynce Kennedy
   c. Susan Brownmiller
   d. Gloria Steinem

15. "We've come a long way. Forty years ago women were playing tennis in floppy hats and funny dresses. Now Bobby Riggs is doing it."

   a. Billie Jean King
   b. Chris Evert
   c. Rosemary Casals
   d. Howard Cosell

(answers on page 177)

Dudes! Who's hangin' in the Oval Office? *(Photo credit: Gerald Ford Library)*

Answer:
From left to right: Billy Preston, George Harrison, President Gerald Ford, Ravi Shankar, and Jack Ford

Music 1

1. It was the top hit single of the entire decade. It was No. 1 for 10 weeks in 1978. You may have tried to put it out of your mind, but if you think really hard, it will all start coming back to you, again and again, over and over. Dare you name it?
2. Who gave us that '70s anthem "Sex and Drugs and Rock and Roll"?
3. Whose career began to go *downhill* when he told *Rolling Stone* in March 1972 that he had tried drugs and liked sex?
4. What was Simon's first hit song without Garfunkel?
5. Who killed Nancy Spungen?
6. Why were record labels owned by Warner Communications boycotted for three years starting in 1976?
7. This 1973 country sensation took up singing and songwriting at the suggestion of his probation officer after he was caught rustling goats in Texas. Who was he?
8. Why, reportedly, did the British group 10cc call itself by that name?
9. On April 29, 1976, he jumped the fence at Graceland in an attempt to meet his idol, Elvis Presley. Despite explaining that he had been on the covers of both *Time* and *Newsweek* the previous October, he was escorted off the grounds by security guards. Who was he?
10. Then, on November 23, 1976, another musician was arrested outside Graceland after shouting, waving a pistol, and demanding to see Elvis. Who was he?
11. John Denver earned a top rating with his 1976 TV special *John Denver and Friend*. Who was the friend?
12. In June 1977, Marvel Comics issued a comic book based on the exploits of this rock group—and even mixed a little blood from group members with the red ink used to print it. What was the group?
13. In 1976 a prominent musician was found guilty of plagiarizing one of his songs from the 1962 hit "He's So Fine." Name the musician and his song.
14. On March 15, 1977, listeners reported to Los Angeles police that something must be wrong at radio station KHJ: DJ Robert W. Morgan had been playing the same song over and over for an hour and a half. What was the name of the song?

15. Last, and certainly not least: Between 1973 and 1979, how many versions of "Tie a Yellow Ribbon 'Round the Ole Oak Tree," originally sung by Tony Orlando and Dawn, were recorded?

    a. 1–250
    b. 251–500
    c. 501–1,000
    d. more than 1,000

(answers on page 177)

Numbers—Culture

Match the correct number to each item.

1. In millions, the number of Happy Face buttons sold in 1971 by New York wholesaler N. G. Slater
2. As of September 1973, the number, in billions, of McDonald's hamburgers sold
3. The number of Ronald McDonalds roaming the country at that time
4. The cost, in dollars, of a Pet Rock nestled in its handy carrying case
5. The maximum number of seconds each act had on *The Gong Show*, if it didn't get gonged first
6. As of March 1977, the number, in millions, of Farrah Fawcett-Majors posters that had been sold
7. The number of weeks Pink Floyd's *Dark Side of the Moon* album remained on the *Billboard* charts after it was released in 1973
8. The percentage of NBC's total profits brought in by *The Tonight Show Starring Johnny Carson* in 1978
9. The percentage of American homes with cable TV as of 1979
10. As of December 1978, the number of countries in which you could see *The Muppet Show*

    a. 45
    b. 132
    c. 17
    d. 5
    e. 5
    f. 20
    g. 20
    h. 106
    i. 12
    j. 50

(answers on page 178)

Sports 1

1. In 1974 Hank Aaron broke Babe Ruth's home-run record of 714. By the time he retired in 1976, how many home runs had Aaron hit?
2. Who was Stan Barrett?
3. In 1974 Evel Knievel, driving a rocket-powered motorcycle, tried to jump over something that no one had ever jumped over before. What was it, and was he successful?
4. In 1973 this NFL team became the first in 30 years to be undefeated and untied in both regular season and play-offs. Name it.
5. Whom did Bobby Fischer defeat in 1972 to become the first world chess champion from the U.S.?
6. Citing improper language and gestures, whom did the Davis Cup committee bar from play in October 1977?
7. What did the number 25 mean to Secretariat?
8. "Most of it is unprintable," he said of his conversations with his baseball. "But the gist of it is, 'Come on now, curve ... we got to curve ...' Or if I need a strike, 'Come on now, get over. You need a strike in the outside corner.'" This Detroit Tigers pitcher won 19 games during his first season, 1976. Who was he?
9. In 1971 icy relations between the U.S. and the People's Republic of China began to thaw as they competed in what sport?
10. In 1978 Ohio State coach Woody Hayes punched a Clemson linebacker during the last few minutes of the Gator Bowl, an action that cost him his job. Whom did he punch?
11. Who were the L.A. Dandelions?
12. Who set a record (of sorts) in professional basketball by destroying two glass backboards in two weeks in 1979?
13. The first black manager of a major league baseball team was hired in the '70s. Who was he, and what team did he manage?
14. Whom did the New York Cosmos hire in 1975 to give new life to soccer in the U.S.?
15. What teams played in the American Basketball Association's last championship game in 1976, and what was the result?

(answers on page 178)

Movies 1

1. Who said, "I'm mad as hell and I'm not going to take it anymore"?
2. At what disco did Tony Manero (John Travolta) compete for the annual $500 dance prize in *Saturday Night Fever*?
3. What movie introduced Sensurround?
4. How did Babs Johnson (Divine) win the title of "filthiest person in the world" in *Pink Flamingos*?
5. What was "Telefon" the code name for?
6. Although *M*A*S*H* was a war movie, on only one occasion are gunshots heard in the film. When?
7. In *Star Wars*, what was the name of Han Solo's (Harrison Ford's) ship?
8. Rudolf Nureyev starred in a 1977 movie about the life of a famous silent screen star. Name it.
9. In *The Last Remake of Beau Geste*, how long was Digby (Marty Feldman) sentenced to jail for stealing the Blue Water Sapphire?
10. Lucille Ball's final film, in 1974, was this disappointing musical. Name it.
11. In *Harry and Tonto*, who was Tonto?
12. What relationship was Daisy Campbell (Barbra Streisand) to Melinda Tentrees in *On a Clear Day You Can See Forever*?
13. How many hours did Smokey (Burt Reynolds) have to get his rig from Georgia to Texarkana and back, and how many cases of Coors was he supposed to return with in *Smokey and the Bandit*?
14. What was Dirty Harry's (Clint Eastwood's) last name?
15. New York City policeman Eddie Egan was the inspiration for what movie hero?

(answers on page 178)

How many days did President Carter keep Menachem Begin and Anwar Sadat sequestered at Camp David before they reached their historic peace agreement in 1978?
(Photo credit: Jimmy Carter Library)

Answer: 13

TV Kids

Zero Population Growth was a big movement in the '70s, but evidently it never arrived in TV-land. Can you sort out which children below were Bradys, Partridges, Waltons, and Bradfords (*Eight Is Enough*)?

Ben	Joannie
Bobby	John Boy
Christopher	Keith
Cindy	Laurie
Danny	Marcia
David	Mary
Elizabeth	Mary Ellen
Elizabeth	Nancy
Erin	Nicholas
Greg	Peter
Jan	Susan
Jason	Tommy
Jim-Bob	Tracy

(answers on page 179)

Richard Nixon

Richard Milhous Nixon. What can you say? He was the best of presidents, he was the worst of presidents. Mostly the latter. He had a long nose and was lucky it didn't grow longer when he lied.

1. Nixon liked this 1970 movie so much that he watched it repeatedly in the White House screening room. What was it?
2. In 1971 Nixon reported $262,385 in income to the IRS. To the nearest thousand, how much did he pay in federal taxes?
3. Nixon was a lawyer, of course. As of 1976, where was he no longer allowed to practice law?
4. What was La Casa Pacifica and where was it?
5. Whom did Julie marry?
6. How about Tricia?
7. Who was Vicky Nixon?
8. What did Nixon like to put on his cottage cheese?
9. Whose 13-year sentence for jury tampering and mail fraud did Nixon commute just in time for Christmas 1971?

10. What did Nixon reportedly do to a portrait of Abraham Lincoln during the last days of his presidency?
11. During those final days, Nixon and Henry Kissinger knelt down on the floor of the Oval Office and did something. What?
12. Where was Nixon when his resignation took effect?
13. To whom did he submit his resignation letter?
14. Where, in 1978, did Nixon make his first public appearance since resigning, to dedicate the Richard Nixon Recreation Center?
15. After his 1972 landslide reelection victory, what did Nixon consider campaigning for?

(answers on page 180)

First Lines 1

Match the first line with the book it came from.

1. "No one remembers her beginnings."
2. "What can you say about a twenty-five-year-old girl who died?"
3. "I can see by my watch, without taking my hand from the left grip of the cycle, that it is eight-thirty in the morning."
4. "The crash of glass made her head throb."
5. "Ashton Hilary Akbar Pelham-Martyn was born in a camp near the crest of a pass in the Himalayas, and subsequently christened in a patent canvas bucket."
6. "There were 117 psychoanalysts on the Pan Am flight to Vienna and I'd been treated by at least six of them."
7. "We were somewhere around Barstow on the edge of the desert when the drugs began to take hold."
8. "The primroses were over."
9. "The gale tore at him and he felt its bite deep within and he knew that if they did not make landfall in three days they would all be dead."

10. "Without warning, in the middle of my thirties, I had a breakdown of nerve."
11. "Amoebae leave no fossils."
12. "Lying prostrate, Serge Duran gaped at Augustus Plebesly who was racing inexorably around the track."
13. "What makes Iago evil? some people ask."
14. "All of us who are not disabled or dumb are able to sing and dance—after a fashion."
15. "Dead."

    a. Watership Down *by Richard Adams*
    b. Fear of Flying *by Erica Jong*
    c. Even Cowgirls Get the Blues *by Tom Robbins*
    d. The Joy of Sex *edited by Alex Comfort*
    e. Mommie Dearest *by Christina Crawford*
    f. The New Centurions *by Joseph Wambaugh*
    g. Rubyfruit Jungle *by Rita Mae Brown*
    h. Shogun *by James Clavell*
    i. Fear and Loathing in Las Vegas *by Hunter S. Thompson*
    j. The Far Pavilions *by M. M. Kaye*
    k. Passages *by Gail Sheehy*
    l. Zen and the Art of Motorcycle Maintenance *by Robert M. Pirsig*
    m. Love Story *by Erich Segal*
    n. Sybil *by Flora Rheta Schreiber*
    o. Play It as It Lays *by Joan Didion*

(answers on page 180)

TV 2

1. In *David Cassidy—Man Undercover*, what was the name of the character that David Cassidy played? (And no, it wasn't "David Cassidy.")
2. Who worked as dock foreman for the Prendergast Tool and Die Company?
3. On the 1978 broadcast of the miniseries *Rescue from Gilligan's Island*, all of the original cast of *Gilligan's Island* returned except one. Who?
4. What was located on a farm near Walnut Grove, Minnesota?
5. Who were Jed "Kid" Curry and Hannibal Heyes?
6. *The Mary Tyler Moore Show* had three spinoffs during the '70s. Name them.
7. Who was Jimmy Joe Jeeter and how did he die?
8. What crime-fighting team reported directly to Governor Philip Gray?
9. On what two unrelated shows was the character Sandy Stockton the lead?
10. Who was the pastor of the Church of What's Happening Now?
11. What was the profession of Mike Brady?
12. Who, on October 11, 1975, was the first host of *Saturday Night Live*?
13. What was the name of the cruise ship on *The Love Boat*?
14. Name the spoof of traditional beauty pageants hosted by Rip Taylor and produced by Chuck Barris.
15. Who were Consuelo Lopez and Kathleen Faverty?

(answers on page 180)

News 2

1. Who, in 1977, presented the Department of Agriculture with his Golden Fleece Award for using taxpayers' money to study how long it took to cook breakfast?
2. It cost 25 cents to produce, sold for $4.35, and caused endless misery to thousands of women in the form of infections, sterilization, birth defects, and even death. What was it?
3. What was the "Twinkie defense"?
4. It was described in a 1975 *Time* magazine cover story as "the greatest and

swiftest transfer of wealth in all history." What was it?

5. Who announced during a "God Bless America Festival" at Yankee Stadium in 1976 that "God has sent me to America in the role of a doctor" to cure the "illness in your home"?

6. What did Patty Hearst's kidnappers demand that her family give to the poor?

7. Two women tried to shoot President Ford on separate occasions during September 1975. One, in a classic case of the pot calling the kettle black, described the other, a Manson family member, as "insane." Who were they?

8. In 1975, 11 people died and 75 were injured when a bomb exploded in the main terminal of what U.S. airport?

9. Who won the 1972 Nobel Peace Prize?

10. President Carter's inflation fighter, Alfred Kahn, was concerned that people were being unduly frightened by the word "inflation." What more soothing word did he use as a substitute?

11. What was the name of the missile system designed to move around on an underground railway, so as to better evade destruction by the Soviets?

12. And what proposed weapon was supposed to kill people but leave buildings intact?

13. What took place at Port Kaituma airstrip?

14. His 1978 lawsuit against the University of California alleged "reverse discrimination" because minority applicants with lower test scores were admitted to medical school and he wasn't. Who was he, and did he win his case?

15. What did the U.S. give back to Japan in 1972?

(answers on page 181)

20 Songs You're Going to Hate Us for Reminding You Of

The performers below may have been relegated to obscurity, but their songs are, unfortunately, not so easy to forget. Yes, you may secretly like one or two—after all, none of us can completely escape the taste for sugarcoated junk that we developed as children. But we can try. See if you can match the song with the artist (and we use that term loosely). WARNING: Reading song titles may trigger endless repetition of bad music in your head.

1. "Love Grows (Where My Rosemary Goes)"
2. "Billy, Don't Be a Hero"
3. "Kung Fu Fighting"
4. "Seasons in the Sun"
5. "Me and You and a Dog Named Boo"
6. "Spirit in the Sky"
7. "Heartbeat, It's a Lovebeat"
8. "The Night Chicago Died"
9. "Play That Funky Music"
10. "In the Summertime"
11. "Escape (The Piña Colada Song)"
12. "Afternoon Delight"
13. "I Like Dreamin'"
14. "Feelings"
15. "Convoy"
16. "Patches"
17. "Teddy Bear"
18. "Hot Child in the City"
19. "Brandy (You're a Fine Girl)"
20. "Chick-a-Boom"

a. *Lobo*
b. *Norman Greenbaum*
c. *Wild Cherry*
d. *The DeFranco Family*
e. *Terry Jacks*
f. *Kenny Nolan*
g. *Paper Lace*
h. *Nick Gilder*
i. *Bo Donaldson and the Heywoods*
j. *Red Sovine*
k. *Clarence Carter*
l. *Carl Douglas*
m. *Rupert Holmes*
n. *Starland Vocal Band*
o. *Looking Glass*
p. *Edison Lighthouse*
q. *Mungo Jerry*
r. *Morris Albert*
s. *C. W. McCall*
t. *Daddy Dewdrop*

(answers on page 182)

Movies 2

1. In the Mel Brooks film *Silent Movie*, there was only one spoken line. What was it, and who said it?
2. Why did Dirty Harry (Clint Eastwood) have the nickname "dirty"?
3. In the horror film *Night of the Lepus*, large, menacing, human-eating creatures wreaked havoc in the Arizona desert. Exactly what kind of creatures were they?
4. Who were the "Human Beings" in *Little Big Man*?
5. What was the name of the boxer with whom Rocky Balboa (Sylvester Stallone) went the distance in *Rocky*?
6. In *Star Wars*, where did Princess Leia (Carrie Fisher) tell Darth Vader that the rebel base was located, and where was it actually located?
7. Who were the first passengers shown boarding *The Magic Christian*?
8. In *Everything You Always Wanted to Know About Sex (But Were Afraid to Ask)*, with whom did Dr. Ross (Gene Wilder) fall in love, and what was unusual about her?
9. What was the full name of the fraternity known as Delta House?
10. This Jules Feiffer film, starring Jack Nicholson, Candice Bergen, and Art Garfunkel, was ruled obscene by the Georgia Supreme Court. Name it.
11. What was Alfred Hitchcock's final movie?
12. Who was the only actor from the film *Alice Doesn't Live Here Anymore* to go on to star in the TV series *Alice*?
13. How did Holly's (Sissy Spacek's) father punish her for running around with Kit (Martin Sheen) in *Badlands*?
14. With whom did Patton (George C. Scott) commune before going into battle?
15. Who wanted to be king of Kafiristan?

(answers on page 182)

Before there was Chelsea, there was Amy.
And before there was Socks, there was this
White House cat. What was its name?
(Hint: The name was four words long.)
(Photo credit: Jimmy Carter Library)

Answer:
Misty Malarky Ying Yang

Quotes 2

Who said:

1. "The '50s had its Marilyn Monroe type. In the '60s everything was straight hair. I guess I'm the '70s woman."

    a. Dolly Parton
    b. Cheryl Tiegs
    c. Diane Keaton
    d. Divine

2. "What Dom Perignon is to champagne, I am to acting. You must realize that I happen to be a particularly good fan of mine."

    a. Erik Estrada
    b. Raquel Welch
    c. Charlton Heston
    d. Truman Capote

3. "My movies were the kind they show in prisons and airplanes, because nobody can leave."

    a. Charles Bronson
    b. Irwin Allen
    c. Burt Reynolds
    d. Tom Laughlin

4. "They'd publish my parking tickets."

    a. Sylvester Stallone
    b. Danielle Steel
    c. Stephen King
    d. Clifford Irving

5. "Many of us allow our children to eat junk, watch junk, listen to junk, talk junk, play with junk, and then we're surprised when they come out to be social junkies."

    a. Jesse Jackson
    b. Ralph Nader
    c. Adelle Davis
    d. Fred Silverman

6. "The United States has passed its historic high point, like so many earlier civilizations."

    a. Fidel Castro
    b. Andrei Gromyko
    c. Muammar Qaddafi
    d. Henry Kissinger

7. "If when the chips are down the world's most powerful nation acts like a pitiful, helpless giant, the forces of totalitarianism and anarchy will threaten free nations and free institutions throughout the world."

    a. *Jimmy Carter*
    b. *Richard Nixon*
    c. *Gerald Ford*
    d. *Big Bird*

8. "We could not simply walk away from an enterprise involving two administrations, five allied countries, and 31,000 American dead as if we were switching a television channel."

    a. *Melvin Laird*
    b. *William Westmoreland*
    c. *Henry Kissinger*
    d. *John Wayne*

9. "Very frankly, any senator who talks about sending American forces into Cambodia ought to lead the charge himself. I'm fed up with old men dreaming up wars for young men to die in—particularly stupid wars of this kind that add nothing to our security."

    a. *Frank Church*
    b. *Jane Fonda*
    c. *George McGovern*
    d. *Edwin Starr*

10. "When men talk about defense, they always claim to be protecting women and children, but they never ask the women and children what they think."

    a. *Pat Schroeder*
    b. *Barbara Jordan*
    c. *Bella Abzug*
    d. *Abigail Van Buren*

11. "I'm working on getting a woman on the Supreme Court as soon as possible."

    a. *Richard Nixon*
    b. *Gerald Ford*
    c. *Jimmy Carter*
    d. *Betty Ford*

12. "Any woman who chooses to behave like a full human being should be warned that the armies of the status quo will treat her as something of a dirty joke; that's their natural and first weapon."

    a. *Gloria Steinem*
    b. *Robin Morgan*
    c. *Bella Abzug*
    d. *Dolly Parton*

13. "If God meant to have homosexuals, he would have created Adam and Bruce."

    a. *Pat Robertson*
    b. *Anita Bryant*
    c. *Oral Roberts*
    d. *Joan Rivers*

14. "If God dislikes gays so much, how come he picked Michelangelo, a known homosexual, to paint the Sistine Chapel ceiling while assigning Anita to go on TV and push orange juice?"

    a. *Art Buchwald*
    b. *Mike Royko*
    c. *Andy Warhol*
    d. *Lily Tomlin*

15. "As far as I'm concerned, being any gender is a drag."

    a. *David Bowie*
    b. *Patti Smith*
    c. *Elton John*
    d. *Liberace*

(answers on page 183)

Boogie Fever

We had it bad. By 1979, according to *Life* magazine, 37 million Americans were dancing at the nation's 10,000 discos. It seemed like another 37 million were making disco records, movies, and TV shows. There was even a disco version of "Hava Nagilah," which leads us to our first question . . .

1. Whose 1975 *Disco Party* album let us get down to that funky Jewish folk-song sound?
2. Listeners swore they heard Donna Summer moan her way through upwards of seven loud orgasms during this 1976 hit song. What was it?

3. Which six of the following were costumes worn by the Village People?

> *doctor*
> *Indian chief*
> *cowboy*
> *leather aficionado*
> *policeman*
> *fireman*
> *knight*
> *lifeguard*
> *soldier*
> *lumberjack*
> *football player*
> *construction worker*

4. Who, in 1979, billed himself as "The Original Disco Man" and made a comeback with the hit "It's Too Funky In Here"?
5. What record quacked its way to platinum in 1976?
6. What was a "disco biscuit"?
7. In what song were we treated to the immortal words, "Here comes DJ Disco Tex, truckin' with his Sex-o-lettes!"
8. In the movie *Love at First Bite*, to what song did Dracula, played by George Hamilton, boogie?

9. The Bee Gees had seven No. 1 singles between 1975 and 1979. Name 'em.
10. The theme from this popular '50s TV show became the basis for a 1977 disco single. What was the show?
11. *Rolling Stone* called this Japanese musical duo "the best-selling female recording act in the world" in 1979. They tried to crack the U.S. market with a disco single, "Kiss in the Dark," in which they sang English phonetically. Who were they?
12. What was *the* New York disco, which attracted such celebrities as Truman Capote, Jackie Onassis, and Miss Lillian Carter—not to mention the eventual suspicion of the IRS, which sent owners Steve Rubell and Ian Schrager to prison for tax evasion and profit skimming?
13. This 1975 Van McCoy single led to a dance craze that had the same name as the song. What was it?
14. Name the tune that was the official theme song of the Pittsburgh Pirates in 1979.
15. Who, exactly, was Karen Lynn Gorney?

(answers on page 183)

Which one's Billy? Too easy? Then fill in the blanks in this Billy Carter quote: "Yes, sir! I'm a real Southern boy. I got a red _____, white _____, and Blue _____ beer."
(Photo credit: Jimmy Carter Library)

Answer:
neck, socks, Ribbon

Watergate Whodunit

Below are the names of 26 people involved, to one degree or another, in Watergate and its aftermath. Some were crooks, some were not. Can you match each person to his role in the affair?

1. Sent Nixon a card wishing him "a speedy recovery from Watergate"
2. CREEP aide and Watergate burglar
3. Presidential appointments secretary, found guilty of perjury
4. White House consultant and Watergate burglar
5. Commerce secretary, pled guilty to campaign law violations
6. Watergate burglar
7. Watergate burglar
8. Watergate burglar
9. Watergate burglar
10. Watergate burglar
11. Chairman of Senate Watergate Committee
12. Chairman of House Judiciary Committee
13. Former attorney general, head of CREEP, later jailed
14. Nixon's counsel during final days of his presidency
15. Rabbi and staunch Nixon defender
16. Messiah and staunch Nixon defender
17. Head of White House dirty tricks unit
18. Nixon chief of staff, jailed for role in coverup
19. Nixon chief domestic advisor, same as above
20. White House counsel, turned state's evidence
21. First Special Prosecutor
22. Second Special Prosecutor
23. "Unindicted co-conspirator," pardoned for role in scandal
24. Chief counsel to Senate Watergate Committee
25. District court judge and bane of Nixon's existence
26. White House aide, pled guilty to coverup

    a. *Samuel Dash*
    b. *H. R. Haldeman*
    c. *Bernard Barker*
    d. *Richard Nixon*
    e. *Dwight Chapin*
    f. *Leon Jaworski*
    g. *Sam Ervin*

h. Sun Myung Moon
i. Maurice Stans
j. James McCord
k. Eugenio Martinez
l. E. Howard Hunt
m. G. Gordon Liddy
n. John Dean
o. Archibald Cox
p. Baruch M. Korff
q. Peter Rodino
r. James St. Clair
s. Egil Krogh, Jr.
t. Jeb Magruder
u. John J. Sirica
v. Virgilio Gonzalez
w. John Mitchell
x. Frank Sturgis
y. John Ehrlichman
z. Idi Amin

(answers on page 184)

Trends 1

1. The first male nude centerfold appeared in the April 1972 issue of *Cosmopolitan*. Who posed for it?
2. Why, in 1977, did the M&M Mars Company stop making red M&Ms?
3. Which state's supreme court ruled in 1975 that it was OK to use marijuana in the privacy of one's own home?
4. What did "est" stand for, and what did Werner Erhard do before he founded it?
5. What was banned from TV on January 1, 1971?
6. Who, in CB lingo, was "First Mama"?
7. In 1972 it surpassed the Model T to become the best-selling car model ever sold. What was it?
8. The U.S. Supreme Court ruled in 1972 that single people in Massachusetts could no longer be prevented from buying what?
9. What was unusual about 1979's Hurricane Bob?
10. What comic strip became the first to win a Pulitzer Prize?
11. Why did attorney Marvin Mitchelson attract the nation's attention in 1979?

12. Fashion-wise, what was the Wedge?
13. It seemed like 1974 was a banner year for shortages. Nine of the following items were in short supply at some point that year. Three were not. Which weren't?

> *black raisins*
> *cardboard boxes*
> *coat hangers*
> *grocery bags*
> *onions*
> *paper clips*
> *pennies*
> *rice*
> *rope*
> *soybeans*
> *toilet paper*
> *toothpaste*

14. Gilbert and Lesley Brown of Bristol, England, had a daughter on July 25, 1978. What was special about her?
15. Who said that a cat could frequently be mistaken for a meat loaf?

(answers on page 184)

Numbers—Relationships

Match the correct number to each item.

1. The number of romance novels written by Barbara Cartland in 1978
2. The amount, in dollars, earned per day by Linda Lovelace for acting in *Deep Throat*
3. As of 1972, the number of states in which homosexual relations were illegal
4. The number of motorists in Scott County, Iowa, who returned their license plates in 1979 because they bore the prefix "GAY"
5. As of November 1972, the percentage of Americans polled who disapproved of marriages between whites and blacks
6. The amount, in dollars, paid by Olga Korbut for her wedding gown, which she bought at a J. C. Penney store in St. Louis in 1976
7. The number of days newlywed couples in the Reverend Sun Myung Moon's Unification Church were required to abstain from sex after getting married in one of those lovely mass ceremonies
8. The percentage increase in the divorce rate between 1970 and 1979

9. The percentage increase in the number of psychologists during the '70s
10. The percentage decrease in the number of barbers

    a. 42
    b. 175
    c. 235
    d. 60
    e. 24
    f. 281
    g. 28
    h. 40
    i. 54
    j. 130

(answers on page 185)

People 2

1. Why was Kentucky Fried Chicken founder Colonel Harlan Sanders sued by the company he'd sold the chain to in 1978?
2. Who was Steven Weed?
3. One of the detractors of this Nixon U.S. Supreme Court nominee said of him, "This nominee presents the most slender credentials of any man put forward in this century." And one of his *supporters* said, "There are a lot of mediocre judges and people and lawyers. They are entitled to a little representation, aren't they?" Name the nominee.
4. Jackie "Tonowanda" Garret, a former female boxer, served as a bodyguard to what heavyweight champion?
5. This religious leader liked to play practical jokes on his friends, such as throwing them into swimming pools, squirting shaving cream in their faces, and closing their heads in car windows. (What a card!) Who was he?
6. In California in 1976, someone put up a $2 million, 24½-mile "running fence" made of nylon and called it art. Who?
7. At the start of this player's last soccer game, he led the stadium's 75,646 fans in a chant of "Love! Love! Love!" Name him.
8. On July 21, 1971, whom did Richard Nixon give the first of the new Eisenhower dollar coins to?
9. When Granville Bishop was arrested in 1973 for firing 17 rifle shots into his TV, what was his explanation?

Just think of the pins as the Senate Watergate Committee. President Nixon goes for a strike in the White House bowling alley. What was his average?
(Photo credit: National Archives)

Answer: 175

10. Whom did singer John Denver call "a god"?

11. In 1975, three days after her divorce from Sonny was final, Cher married again. Whom did she marry, and how long did the marriage last?

12. John Draper was arrested by the FBI in 1972 and charged with being "Captain Crunch," the head of an illegal network of "phone phreaks," whose main purpose in life was to outwit the Bell Telephone System. Just how did Captain Crunch get his name?

13. Who was known as the "Sweetheart of the Silent Majority"?

14. What world leader chose as her chief adviser a former police official who claimed to have co-authored a book on the occult with the Archangel Gabriel?

15. This Carter-administration diplomat called former presidents Richard Nixon and Gerald Ford "racists" and said on a trip overseas that the Russians were "the worst racists in the world." Name him.

(answers on page 185)

Disaster Movies

Below are 15 disaster movie plots. Can you match them to their titles? And can you pick out the one fake?

1. Blizzard closes airport, nut with bomb in briefcase terrorizes plane
2. Hijacked plane sinks into ocean, nervous passengers avoid annoying air pocket until rescue
3. Flighty flight attendant forced to fly disabled jumbo jet through mountainous terrain until Charlton Heston is airlifted through gaping hole in cockpit
4. Plane is shot down with missiles and crash-lands in the Alps, thus delaying Martha Raye's needed kidney transplant
5. Champagne and saltwater flow as tidal wave capsizes cruise ship on New Year's Eve
6. Bomb on ocean liner and $1 million ransom demand that better be met—or the sharks will be eatin' good tonight!
7. Fire in skyscraper kills half of Hollywood, but O. J. Simpson rescues the kitty

8. Exposure to deadly virus *and* train ride over rickety bridge—maybe flying really is the safest way to travel
9. Terrorists plan spectacular halftime show at Super Bowl, using explosive-laden Goodyear blimp to kill president, fans, and insufferable sports commentators
10. African killer bees attack Texas, befuddle Henry Fonda, and cause nuclear power plant to explode
11. Cargo ship releases African killer bees into New Orleans at Mardi Gras, turning Fat Tuesday into Sore Wednesday
12. Experimental bees from Brazil attack pleasant-smelling Pasadena Rose Parade, then negotiate with U.S. government to end pollution
13. Foot-long mutant cockroaches emerge after earthquake and spit fire from their anal regions at Riverside, California.
14. They're hungry, they have pointy teeth, and they're only pretending to be sleeping
15. Watch out, New York, something bigger than an apple is headed your way!

a. *The Bees*
b. *The Towering Inferno*
c. *The Concorde—Airport '79*
d. *The Poseidon Adventure*
e. *Possums!*
f. *Airport '77*
g. *Bug*
h. *The Swarm*
i. *Airport 1975*
j. *Black Sunday*
k. *Meteor*
l. *Juggernaut*
m. *The Cassandra Crossing*
n. *Airport*
o. *The Savage Bees*

(answers on page 186)

Presidents for Life

The '70s were a good time to set yourself up as president for life, murder an archbishop or two, decorate yourself with lots of medals, and plunder the national treasury. But many of the era's most infamous dictators didn't last to the end of the decade, 1979 being a particularly bad year for megalomania.

1. What did Idi Amin Dada claim President Nixon was trying to export to Uganda?
2. Amin and Mobutu Sese Seko, Zaire's president for life, decided in 1973 to change the names of two lakes along their borders. What were Lake Albert and Lake Edward renamed?
3. Whom did Amin have hacked to death and stuffed in the trunk of a car?
4. On a lighter note: What 1971 weeklong party featured 25,000 bottles of wine, quail eggs and caviar from Maxim's of Paris, and 500 guests, including Vice President Agnew, Princess Grace and Prince Rainier of Monaco, and Marshal Tito of Yugoslavia? (Hint: The guests were housed in tents.)
5. What regime hired the U.S. advertising firm of J. Walter Thompson to counter criticism of its record of torture, executions, and other crimes?
6. So beloved was he by his people that he took to speaking in a bulletproof glass booth shortly before his overthrow in 1979, which ended 43 years of rule by his family. Who was he?
7. According to *Saturday Night Live*, who was still dead, at least as of 1976?
8. Shortly after this president declared martial law in 1972, his wife was wounded in a politically inspired knife attack. A plastic surgeon was brought in from the U.S. to fix her face. Name the husband, or the wife, or both.
9. In 1976 he imported 450 pounds of rose petals and 1.5 tons of fireworks for a ceremony in which he put a $5 million crown on his head and declared himself "the world's first socialist emperor." By the time that residents of the impoverished Central African Empire deposed him three years later, he had been accused of cannibalism and mass murder, among other things. Who was he?
10. In 1972 author Frederick Forsyth recruited mercenaries and purchased arms in an attempt to overthrow the despotic government of what small African nation?
11. What best-selling book did Forsyth write after the plan fell through?
12. In 1976 this dictator ordered his embassies throughout the world to smuggle in hashish and duty-free cigarettes and vodka and to sell them to boost his

nation's foreign exchange. Who was he?

13. Jean-Claude "Baby Doc" Duvalier became Haiti's president for life in 1971 upon whose death?

14. In 1979 the deposed Shah of Iran was passed from country to country like a hot potato. Name the six nations that housed him, however briefly, after his flight from Iran on January 16.

15. After assuming power in 1975, he ordered everyone to leave his nation's capital and till the fields. Within four years his regime had killed one-fifth of the country's population. Who was he, what was the country, and what did his regime rename the country?

(answers on page 186)

TV 3

1. What was the name of the dog on *The Brady Bunch*?

2. On *Columbo*, what was Lieutenant Columbo's first name?

3. Detective Ron Harris, on *Barney Miller*, wrote a sensational novel about police work while working at the 12th Precinct. What was his book called?

4. What U.S. President appeared on *Saturday Night Live*?

5. Who married Lieutenant Colonel Donald Penobscott?

6. Where was *Room 222* located?

7. The South, especially Georgia, became trendy after Carter's election. Name the program that was set in Clinton Corners, Georgia, "just down the road from Plains."

8. What type of car did Dave Starsky drive in *Starsky and Hutch*?

9. Who were *The Snoop Sisters*, and what did they do for a living?

10. Where did Laverne De Fazio and Shirley Feeney work?

11. Name Kwai Chang Caine's two teachers on *Kung Fu*.

12. The longest continuously running TV police show ran throughout the entire decade of the '70s. Name it.

13. Who was the mascot of Squad 51 on *Emergency*?

14. Who was Ficus?

15. Name the paper that *Lou Grant* was city editor of.

(answers on page 187)

Songs 2

From these first lines, name the songs and the people who performed them.

1. "You walked into the party like you were walking onto a yacht."
2. "Jeremiah was a bullfrog, was a good friend of mine."
3. "Sittin' in a park in Paris, France."
4. "Cowboys ain't easy to love and they're harder to hold."
5. "There is a young cowboy, he lives on the range."
6. "I was born in the wagon of a travelin' show."
7. "If a picture paints a thousand words, then why can't I paint you?"
8. "I've paid my dues, time after time."
9. "You've got me runnin', goin' out of my mind."
10. "Well, I dreamed I saw the knights in armor coming, sayin' something about a queen."
11. "Raven hair and ruby lips, sparks fly from her fingertips."
12. "Right now, ha, ha, I am an anti-Christ."
13. "Jesus loves the little children, all the little children of the world."
14. "Who can take a sunrise, sprinkle it with dew?"
15. "I'll light the fire . . ."

(answers on page 188)

Movies 3

1. What was the name of Arnold Schwarzenegger's first film, and how was he billed?
2. In *Alien*, who was Jones?
3. This 1970 Florence Henderson extravaganza about the life of Norwegian composer Edvard Grieg featured 25 songs, 45 musical numbers, and Edward G. Robinson as a cute little piano salesman. Name it.
4. What was the highest grossing movie of the decade?
5. In *The Tin Drum*, at what age did Oskar (David Bennent) decide to stop growing?
6. Name the 1976 film that Woody Allen starred in but that he neither wrote nor directed.
7. What did the female drug kingpin say in horror when Foxy Brown (Pam

Grier) presented her with a jar containing her boyfriend's penis in *Foxy Brown*?

8. In *Nashville*, Barbara Jean (Ronee Blakley) was assassinated at a rally for Hal Phillip Walker. What party was he the presidential candidate for?

9. Robert De Niro played a taxi driver once before his famous role in *Taxi Driver*. Name the 1971 movie in which he drove a gypsy cab.

10. In the 1976 remake of *King Kong*, what astrological sign did Dwan (Jessica Lange) tell King Kong that she was? And what sign did she think he was?

11. What team did Moses Guthrie (Julius Erving) play for in *The Fish That Saved Pittsburgh*?

12. Where did the humans and the aliens have their final close encounter in *Close Encounters of the Third Kind*?

13. In *American Graffiti*, what movie was playing at the local theater?

14. What did it mean when Johnny Hooker (Robert Redford) and Henry Gondorff (Paul Newman) rubbed their noses in *The Sting*?

15. What actors played *The Thing With Two Heads*, in which a white bigot's head was transplanted onto a black man's body?

(answers on page 188)

World News

1. While Americans celebrated their Bicentennial on July 4, 1976, Israeli commandos raided an airport in Uganda and freed 103 hostages held by pro-Palestinian hijackers. What was the name of the airport?

2. Several months later Egypt tried a similar rescue operation with more limited success. Where did that rescue take place?

3. In 1977 a black civil-rights leader died in a South African prison, supposedly of an accidental "brain injury." Who was he?

4. What Italian statesman was kidnapped and killed by the Red Brigades in 1978?

5. Where was Democracy Wall?

6. What unusual gift did former Argentinian dictator Juan Perón receive while in exile in Spain in 1971?

Depicted here are three felons and an unindicted co-conspirator. Name them.
(Photo credit: National Archives)

7. Name the great-grandson of Queen Victoria who was assassinated on his boat by the IRA in 1979.
8. What stopped service in 1977 after 85 years of operation?
9. During Leonid Brezhnev's six-hour speech to the 24th Communist Party Congress in 1971, applauding delegates leapt to their feet several times and shouted which one of the following:

   a. *Let's go! Five Year Plan! Let's go!*
   b. *Glory! Glory!*
   c. *So-cial-ism! So-cial-ism!*
   d. *We're Number One! We're Number One!*

10. Comrades, what festival of anti-socialist hooliganism did Soviet police destroy with bulldozers and high-pressure water hoses in 1974?
11. Name the Saudi king assassinated in 1975 by his deranged nephew.
12. Who, in 1970, became the world's first freely elected Marxist president, despite CIA attempts to bribe his nation's congress into nullifying his election?

13. What was the name of the lost tribe of "Stone Age" people found in a remote Philippine rain forest in 1971?
14. What was the Patriotic Front?
15. What bloody 1975–76 invasion by a U.S. ally resulted in an estimated 100,000 deaths—and repeated abstentions by the U.S. on United Nations resolutions condemning the action?

(answers on page 189)

Real Shows? 1

During the '70s there was a secret hideaway near Los Angeles where monkeys with typewriters were assigned the job of writing plots for TV shows. Below are nine of their works, which actually aired, and one fake, written by a human at a computer. Which one is the fake, and what were the names of the real shows?

1. While tracking down the gang responsible for a series of gold shipment thefts during the 1880s, the Cheyenne marshal discovers an underground city

peopled by advanced space aliens. Thorval, the aliens' despotic leader, uses the stolen gold to power a mind control device that enslaves most of his compatriots. For the rest of the series, the marshal struggles to stop the gold thefts and free the enslaved aliens.

2. Dracula is back, this time in San Francisco where he teaches a course in European history at a local college (a night course, naturally). What a coincidence: Professor von Helsing's grandson, Kurt, just happens to be in the same locale.

3. In this comedy, a familyless hairdresser decides to recruit some relatives by—what else?—placing a classified ad in the newspaper. From the respondents she chooses a con-man husband, a feisty, blind grandfather, a tap-dancing daughter, and a son whose ambition is to fly like a bird.

4. Under the oppression of the British "system," young, long-haired, under-30 rebels form the Yankee Doodle Society in Pennsylvania, 1777. Their goal is to overthrow the "system" by spying for the Americans and harassing the British.

5. After suffering a burst of radiation from the sun during a top-secret flight, a pilot discovers that he can make himself tiny at will. He and the government decide to use his newfound power to fight terrorists and other evildoers. Unfortunately, his miniature, specially constructed airplane sometimes draws the unwanted attention of the family cat.

6. The 20-year-old hero of this show spends most of his time searching for his real parents. The problem: He was raised in the forest by wolves and feels uneasy in areas populated by humans.

7. A husband's spirit enters his wife's body and the wife's spirit enters her husband's body when a magical statue grants their idle wish to change places. They spend the rest of the series trying to get the statue to switch them back while they struggle to pass for one another. This is particularly difficult since she's a dainty executive in the cosmetics industry and he's a cigar-smoking sportswriter.

8. Passengers take a train trip back into the past, where they can disembark and change the decisions that caused

them to become so miserable that they needed to get on the train and go back into the past in the first place.

9. In this sitcom, set in a small Midwestern town, the beloved mayor, a widower, has two troublesome children: His daughter is a feminist civil-rights lawyer and his son is a hippie. Whenever things start to get out of control, which is guaranteed to happen once per episode, the mayor breaks into song.

10. A scientist is drawn into a strange "time and space warp" in the Bermuda Triangle, where he encounters a survivor of Atlantis, a scientist from the 1960s who works with androids, a young present-day psychic, and a 23rd-century telepath. The series centers on their efforts to return to their respective times without getting on each other's nerves too much.

(answers on page 189)

Women 2

1. What did Lillian Hellman, Billie Jean King, Lee Grant, Barbara Tuchman, and Judy Collins have in common?

2. When Congress extended the deadline for ratification of the ERA by 39 months in 1978, how many votes short of ratification was the amendment?

3. Which was the first Western Hemisphere nation to be headed by a woman?

4. Who is credited with saying "Today a woman without a man is like a fish without a bicycle"?

5. A year after *Roe v. Wade*, Dr. Kenneth Edelin, the black chief resident in obstetrics and gynecology at Boston City Hospital, was indicted for the "death" of a fetus that was legally aborted. What did his jury—which included 9 men, 10 Catholics, and 12 whites—rule?

6. Margaret Hasselman, a lobby attendant in a Manhattan office building, was told by her boss to wear a special Bicentennial uniform—a red, white, and blue poncho, blue dancer's

panties, and white high heels. What happened when she refused?

7. In 1979 a woman was finally portrayed on a widely circulated piece of American currency. Who was the woman, and why was the currency not popular?

8. Richard Nixon had declared himself strongly opposed to abortion. Of his four appointees to the U.S. Supreme Court, how many voted against *Roe* v. *Wade*?

9. Why was Debbie Shook stripped of her Miss North Carolina title by the state Jaycees in 1979?

10. By the end of the decade, all branches of the U.S. armed services had promoted at least one woman to the rank of admiral or general. Which was the last branch to do so?

11. Whom did Jimmy Carter fire as co-chair of the National Advisory Committee for Women in 1979, causing 26 of the 40 members to resign in protest?

12. Which of the following was *not* an anti-feminist organization during the '70s?

Women Who Want to Be Women
League of Housewives
American Women Are Richly
  Endowed
Females Opposed to Equality
Family, Liberty and God
Men Our Masters
The Pussy Cat League

13. What dubious honor did the University of Maryland have in 1970?

14. Why did a prisoner file suit when Joan Wyatt was hired as the first woman prison guard in a maximum security prison for men in 1973?

15. In 1971 Erin Prizzey of London, England, founded Chiswick Women's Aid, the first place of its kind in the world. What was it?

(answers on page 190)

Remember the days before Watergate, when we had faith in politicians and little children looked up to them? Speaking of which, who said, "The average American is just like the child in the family"? *(Photo credit: National Archives)*

Answer:
Richard Nixon

Watergate Quotes

Supply the missing word(s) from memory, then match the quote to its source from the names listed below.

1. "I want you all to _____ it."
2. "Once the _____ is out of the tube, it's hard to get it back in."
3. "This is the operative statement. The others are _____."
4. "We have a _____ within, close to the presidency, that is growing."
5. "Let others _____ in Watergate; we are going to do our job."
6. "I think we ought to let him hang there. Let him _____ slowly, slowly in the _____."
7. "I'm not going to comment from the White House on a _____-_____ burglary attempt."
8. "What did the president _____ and when did he _____ it?"
9. "I am totally unconcerned about anything other than getting the job done. . . . I would walk over my _____ if necessary."
10. "Our long national _____ is over."

John Dean
John Ehrlichman
Richard Nixon (2 quotes)
Gerald Ford
Howard Baker
Ronald Ziegler (2 quotes)
H. R. Haldeman
Charles Colson

(answers on page 191)

TV 4

1. Besides the bionic men, the bionic woman, and the bionic boy, who else was bionic?
2. When was *Saturday Night Live* not live?
3. When *Columbo* ended its run, a new mystery series featuring his wife began, starring Kate Mulgrew. Although it was on the air less than a year, this series had three separate titles and, by the end, the lead character was no longer Columbo's wife. What were the three names of the show?

4. Who was Wo Fat?
5. What presidential relative put in an appearance on *Hee Haw Honeys*?
6. What were the two things that Jim Rockford said he wouldn't do for money, on *The Rockford Files*?
7. Who said "Good night and good news" at the end of each of his newscasts?
8. Before *All in the Family*, Sally Struthers appeared as a regular on what comedy variety show?
9. Who worked for *The New York Herald*?
10. What was the "something extra" that Sally Burton had on *The Girl With Something Extra*?
11. Before this program featuring a gay character even aired, ABC received 32,000 letters about it—and all but nine of them were against the show. It went on the air anyway and settled in for a 3½-year run. Name it.
12. What detective series character was called "The Maestro" by Sergeant Velie and "Junior" by reporter Frank Flannigan?
13. Name the famous poet who played Nyo Boto in the miniseries *Roots*?
14. Who were Mike Evans and Damon Evans?

15. What did Dr. Paul Lochner do for a living (and "doctor" doesn't count)?

(answers on page 191)

Books 1

1. This book, in which one of the characters says, "The Pulitzer is for the birds," went on to win the Pulitzer Prize for fiction in 1976. Name it.
2. Who was Juan Matus?
3. Why did some people say that David Rorvik was perpetrating a hoax?
4. Name the book that was banned from both the Cedar Lake, Indiana, high school in 1976, and the Eldon, Missouri, high school in 1977 for containing such words as "horny" and "slut."
5. Who were *The Boys of Summer*?
6. The campaign "Don't buy books from crooks" was directed against which 1978 best-seller?
7. *The Sensuous Woman* was written by J, but who wrote *The Sensuous Man*?
8. The author of this popular best-seller admitted that he had plagiarized from a book called *The African*, by Harold

Courlander. Name the author and his best-seller.

9. What was unusual about the author of *Murder Mystery 1*?

10. Why was Philip Agee's former employer upset when he took up writing?

11. What was the best-selling nonfiction book of the decade?

12. Name the prolific author whose 1979 autobiography, *In Memory Yet Green*, was his 200th book.

13. In the children's book *Sylvester and the Magic Pebble*, Sylvester, a young donkey, turns himself into a stone with the aid of a wish-granting pebble, which leads his worried parents to ask all the other animals in town if they've seen him. This inoffensive-sounding book was the subject of protests by citizen and police groups in more than a dozen states. What was there about this Caldecott Medal–winning book that caused such controversy?

14. Who wrote a novel about the "insane" career of President Trick E. Dixon?

15. Why did Jacqueline Kennedy Onassis resign from her job at Viking Press in 1977?

(answers on page 192)

Who Did What? 1

1. Juan Valdez
2. Lisa Halaby
3. Leo Ryan
4. Oliver Sipple
5. Elizabeth McAlister
6. Chris Chubbuck
7. Stephen Bingham
8. Megan Marshak
9. Daniel Gearhart
10. Margo St. James
11. Shirley Hufstedler
12. George Willig
13. John Schmitz
14. James Browning
15. Elizabeth Seton

a. *Person accused of plotting to kidnap Henry Kissinger*

b. *Commentator who shot self to death on TV*

c. *Person who deflected gun pointed toward President Ford by Sara Jane Moore*

d. *Congressman murdered at Jonestown*

e. *American who married Jordan's King Hussein in 1978*

f. *U.S. mercenary executed in Angola despite plea from President Ford*

g. *First American to be canonized, in 1975*

h. *First secretary of the Department of Education*

i. *Last American evacuated from Saigon*

j. *Assistant who discovered that Nelson Rockefeller had died*

k. *Person who climbed New York's World Trade Center in 1978*

l. *Attorney accused of smuggling gun into San Quentin, triggering the prison's bloodiest day, in 1971*

m. *U.S. attorney who prosecuted Patty Hearst*

n. *Founder of prostitutes' rights group, COYOTE*

o. *Presidential nominee of the American Party in 1972*

(answers on page 193)

Politics

1. Whom would Ronald Reagan have chosen as his running mate had he won the GOP nomination in 1976?
2. After he defeated Reagan, whom did Gerald Ford choose?
3. What presidential candidate considered moving to England after losing the election?
4. What famous politician gave hecklers the finger?
5. Who headed "Democrats for Nixon" in 1972?
6. Who was George McGovern's first running mate, and why was he dumped from the ticket?
7. Who said, "I'm not embarrassed at all to be George McGovern's seventh choice for vice president"?
8. And who, for extra points in the Get-A-Life Hall of Fame, were the first six?
9. What presidential candidate announced that he wanted to "protect the earth, serve the people, and explore the universe"?
10. Slogan-wise, who was "Right from the start"? Whom did we need "Now, more than ever"? And who was "A leader, for a change"?

11. Who was the runner-up in presidential balloting at the 1976 Democratic National Convention?
12. Why did Edmund Muskie break down and cry during the 1972 New Hampshire primary?
13. Why did Gerald Ford and Jimmy Carter stand mute at their podiums for more than twenty minutes during their first debate?
14. What independent antiwar candidate for president remarked after his loss in 1972, "Well, after all, I only won two fewer states than McGovern"?
15. What convention voted down pro-choice and gay-rights planks in 1972?

(answers on page 193)

Numbers—Disasters

Match the correct number to each item.

1. The number of people who died in the 1971 Los Angeles earthquake
2. Of the 11 guards killed while being held hostage at the Attica, New York, state prison in 1971, the number shot by attacking state troopers
3. The number of Americans who died liberating the 39 crew members of the *Mayaguez*
4. The number of people who died at Jonestown
5. The number of Israeli athletes killed by terrorists at the 1972 Munich Olympics
6. The number of people who died from Legionnaire's Disease
7. The number of cases of Swine Flu reported in the U.S. during the much-predicted "epidemic" of 1976
8. The number of people infected with the rare, paralytic Guillain-Barre Syndrome after receiving Swine Flu shots
9. The number of feet high-wire acrobat Karl Wallenda fell in 1978 before crashing into a taxicab
10. The payment, in thousands of dollars, offered by the *San Francisco Examiner*

for a piece of Skylab if delivered within 48 hours of its fall to Earth

    a. *6*
    b. *11*
    c. *914*
    d. *62*
    e. *535*
    f. *38*
    g. *10*
    h. *10*
    i. *34*
    j. *100*

(answers on page 194)

Movies 4

1. What was the first X-rated feature length cartoon?
2. Who left home to find his fortune with this advice: "The Lord loves a working man," "Don't trust whitey," and "See a doctor and get rid of it"?
3. What movie took place at the Psycho-Neurotic Institute for the Very, Very Nervous?
4. Name the movie in which Clint Eastwood made his directorial debut.
5. When this Paul Newman hockey film played in Asia, its title was translated as *The Cursing, Roughhouse Rascal Who Plays Dirty.* What was its American title?
6. In *La Cage aux Folles*, what was Albin's (Michael Serrault's) stage name?
7. This Woody Allen film was the first in which he didn't star and was also his first drama. Name it.
8. What piece of classical music figured prominently in the movie *10*?
9. Meryl Streep made her screen debut in what film?
10. In *The Black Bird*, the 1975 parody of *The Maltese Falcon*, two of the actors from the original *Falcon* appeared playing their same characters. Name the actors.
11. What was the first name of Holmes's (George C. Scott's) Dr. Watson in *They Might Be Giants*?
12. Bob Dylan appeared in this film, and his score included the song "Knockin' on Heaven's Door." Name the movie.
13. What town did *McCabe and Mrs. Miller* live in?

The Imperial President meets The King: When Elvis Presley visited the White House in 1970, President Nixon made him an honorary special agent in the war on drugs. What did Elvis give Nixon in return? *(Photo credit: National Archives)*

Answer:
A wood-handled revolver and silver bullets

14. Name the "bleeding-heart" liberal, played by Charles Bronson, who had a change of heart about criminal justice after his family was attacked by thugs in *Death Wish*.
15. What was the name of the dyspeptic nuclear power plant in *The China Syndrome*?

(answers on page 194)

People 3

1. A 15-year-old religious leader rented the Houston Astrodome in 1973, expecting the arrival of 100,000 followers and aliens from outer space. Who was he?
2. During the Watergate scandal, who was known as "Mr. Clean"?
3. After she was kidnapped, Patty Hearst denounced her parents and changed her name. To what?
4. Who completed the first transcontinental hot air balloon flight on November 6, 1973, after having touched down each night to rest in his motor home, which had been conveniently driven behind him?
5. What photo made Mary Vecchio famous?
6. Tawny Godin, Miss America of 1975, lost an estimated $20,000 in personal appearance fees during her reign. Why?
7. Although not usually thought of as a film director, this person's movie, *Fly*, drew a standing ovation at the Cannes Film Festival in 1971. In the film, a fly, seen close-up, explores the nude body of a woman. Name the director.
8. Who was Jack Rosenberg?
9. Perhaps he was only trying to spend Christmas with the Fords. . . . How did Marshall Fields illegally enter the White House grounds on Christmas morning 1974?
10. Who was Dora Bloch?
11. Agnes Gonxha Bojaxhiu won the Nobel Peace Prize in 1979. By what name was she better known?
12. Clayton Moore had been doing something harmless for 30 years, something that a Los Angeles Superior Court judge ruled in August 1979 he could no longer do. What was it?

13. Who was known as the "Steel Magnolia"?
14. What 64-year-old, pipe-smoking woman, elected to the House in 1974, was the inspiration for the *Doonesbury* character Lacey Davenport?
15. Whose doctoral dissertation was entitled "An Integration of the Visual Media via Fat Albert and the Cosby Kids Into the Elementary School Curriculum as a Teaching Aid and Vehicle to Achieve Increased Learning"?

(answers on page 194)

True Or False? 2

Eight of the following 10 items are true. Can you ferret out the two fakes?

1. Sara Jane Moore was a paid informant for the federal Bureau of Alcohol, Tobacco and Firearms who, on the day before she shot at President Ford, helped a federal agent build a case against the man who sold her the gun.
2. In 1978 there was a movement in California to "Save the Anchovies."
3. *The Muppet Show* was removed from Turkish TV during Ramadan 1979 because Miss Piggy, being a pig, was considered by many Muslim viewers to be unclean.
4. Tennessee State Senator Fred Berry submitted a bill in 1976 that would have named a state fossil, but withdrew it after colleagues amended it to make *him* the official state fossil.
5. Noted economist John Kenneth Galbraith proposed that all national boundaries be redrawn to the size and shape of North Dakota so that people would be forced to learn to live with one another.
6. *Jonathan Livingston Seagull* was first classified as nonfiction by booksellers.
7. During his final days in office, Richard Nixon took to sitting in his private study and listening, repeatedly, to "Send in the Clowns."
8. In New York in 1975 a company ran billboard ads for Jesus Jeans that featured a picture of a woman's derriere in very short cutoffs and the slogan "He who loves me follows me."

9. Besides planting a red flag, Yuri Grechko, the first Soviet cosmonaut to walk on the moon, left a portrait of Leonid Brezhnev and a copy of *Das Kapital*.

10. Andy Anderson of Twin Falls, Idaho, celebrated the Bicentennial with a new pair of red, white, and blue dentures that also proclaimed "1976" in red and white enamel whenever he smiled.

(answers on page 195)

Music 2

1. What British group, scheduled to appear on *Saturday Night Live* in 1977, was denied entry into the U.S. on grounds of moral turpitude?

2. Who went on the show in their place and annoyed NBC brass by singing "Radio Radio," a song criticizing the broadcasting business, which network officials had told him not to sing?

3. Three Dog Night had five No. 1 hits in the '70s. Name 'em. (Hint: "One," their first big hit and "the loneliest number that you'll ever do," topped the charts in 1969.)

4. Who were Joyce Vincent Wilson and Thelma Hopkins?

5. Name the 1970 Merle Haggard hit that criticized long hair, pot smoking, and draft-card burning.

6. Who, in October of that year, urged that rock lyrics be screened and that those urging drug use be banned?

7. Why did the Newport Jazz Festival relocate to New York City in 1971?

8. In "Angel," Aretha Franklin sang about a talk with her sister, who also happened to have written the song. What was her sister's name?

9. What 1978 LP broke all sales records to become the most popular album of all time?

10. From what 1979 hit song did Rod Stewart donate the royalties to UNICEF?

11. Whom was Carly Simon supposedly singing about in "You're So Vain"? (And no, it wasn't the guy who did the backup vocals.)

12. What was the first Western rock band to play at the Pyramids?

13. Before whose picture did Bob Marley and the Wailers generally perform, and why?
14. Speculation abounded that this performer and California Governor Jerry Brown would get married during a jaunt to Kenya in 1979, but they returned from Africa separately. Who was Brown's companion?
15. In 1976 police spent three hours rummaging through this performer's California home and found less than one ounce of marijuana. Whose house was it?

(answers on page 195)

TV 5

1. What TV kids sang the song "Sunshine Day"?
2. Who was Chuckles the Clown, and how did he die?
3. This show, produced by disaster mogul Irwin Allen, although not supposed to be a disaster program, did manage in its seven-month run to feature a volcanic eruption, a tidal wave, an earthquake, a typhoon, and an animal attack. Name the show.
4. What was the name of Mr. Bill's dog?
5. What show had "I Am Woman" as its theme song?
6. How much did Jim Rockford charge for his services on *The Rockford Files*?
7. Name the two actors who played Kunta Kinte on *Roots*.
8. On *The Love Boat*, what was Gopher's real name?
9. This Neil Simon play became a TV series with an all-black cast. Name it.
10. Actress Nancy Walker was a *regular* on four TV programs during the '70s. Name them.
11. What happened to the program *James at 15* when James Hunter lost his virginity?
12. How did Sally McMillan die?
13. Who were the Cylons?
14. What business was George Jefferson in?
15. Who were the detectives on *Barney Miller* during its first season?

(answers on page 196)

Between 1974 and 1978, Donny and Marie Osmond put out six LPs, now readily available in Goodwill stores throughout the nation. Name any or all of their album titles.

Answer:
I'm Leaving It All Up to You, Make the World Go Away, Donny and Marie, New Seasons, Winning Combination, and Goin' Coconuts

Most Valuable Players

We could have asked you to name the winners of each year's World Series, but that would have been too . . . easy? So, instead, we'll present you with this mixed-up list of series MVPs. Your job is to figure out in what year each man was voted MVP, then, from memory, name the team he played for.

1.	1970	*Reggie Jackson*
2.	1971	*Bucky Dent*
3.	1972	*Pete Rose*
4.	1973	*Gene Tenace*
5.	1974	*Johnny Bench*
6.	1975	*Willie Stargell*
7.	1976	*Roberto Clemente*
8.	1977	*Brooks Robinson*
9.	1978	*Rollie Fingers*
10.	1979	*Reggie Jackson*

(answers on page 197)

News 3

1. What song did the People's Liberation Army band play to welcome President Nixon to Peking's Great Hall on February 21, 1972?
2. What U.S. company admitted in 1975 that it had paid $22 million in bribes to officials of foreign governments to gain lucrative aerospace contracts?
3. Name the stripper who went for an unexpected dip in Washington, D.C.'s Tidal Basin in 1974 and the congressman whose career came to an end because of his association with her. (Perhaps this ditty printed in *The Wall Street Journal* at the time will help: "She was only a stripper from the Silver Slipper, but she had her ways and means.")
4. What came as a rude surprise to Evelyn and Herbert Giglotto of Collinsville, Illinois, on the night of April 13, 1973?
5. What, besides mail, did California attorney Paul Morantz find in his mailbox in October 1978?
6. A march by neo-Nazis through this predominantly Jewish Chicago suburb

created quite an uproar in 1977. Where did it take place?

7. Name the American communist leader who, in 1972, was acquitted of murder, kidnapping, and criminal conspiracy charges resulting from a 1970 Marin County, California, courthouse shootout.

8. To what celebrity's Palm Springs compound did Spiro Agnew retreat after being forced to resign?

9. It was, the Supreme Court ruled in 1971, "administratively awkward, inconvenient and even bizarre"—but nonetheless constitutional. What was it?

10. He was sentenced to 25 life terms for the murder of 25 migrant farmworkers in California in 1970–71. Who was he?

11. On November 14, 1976, the Plains, Georgia, Baptist Church voted to drop its 11-year-old ban on what?

12. Who was Tongsun Park?

13. Why did Disneyland call out its armed guards and close the park early on August 6, 1970?

14. Whose face graced the front of the 2.9 billion gasoline ration coupons printed in 1974 by the U.S. government but never used?

15. What was unusual about the worst disaster in commercial aviation history, which involved two jetliners in the Canary Islands in 1977?

(answers on page 197)

Enemies List

Twenty of the people listed below were on President Nixon's Enemies List. Twenty were not. Who was *not* on the list?

Bella Abzug	John V. Lindsay
Muhammad Ali	Rich Little
Rona Barrett	Mary McGrory
Warren Beatty	Steve McQueen
Leonard Bernstein	George Meany
Johnny Carson	Walter Mondale
Carol Channing	Edmund Muskie
Shirley Chisholm	Joe Namath
Alistair Cooke	Paul Newman
Bill Cosby	Gregory Peck
Henry Fonda	William Proxmire
Jane Fonda	Tony Randall
Peter Fonda	Rob Reiner
David Frye	Daniel Schorr

J. William Fulbright   *Sargent Shriver*
Elliott Gould   *Tom Snyder*
Hubert Humphrey   *Barbra Streisand*
Henry Jackson   *Sander Vanocur*
Ethel Kennedy   *Gore Vidal*
Norman Lear   *George Wallace*

(answers on page 198)

Movies 5

1. What did the Italian-American Civil Rights League successfully persuade the producer of *The Godfather* to keep out of the film?
2. In *Star Wars*, what was the name of Princess Leia's (Carrie Fisher's) home planet, which was destroyed by the Death Star?
3. What did Travis Bickle do for a living?
4. In *Deliverance*, who didn't survive the canoe trip?
5. Mae West made her final film in 1978. Name it.
6. What was the name of the high school in *Rock 'n' Roll High School*?

7. Tom Laughlin became something of a cult figure for his portrayal of this peace-loving, karate-chopping Native American "half-breed." What was his character called?
8. Who comprised Sgt. Pepper's band in the movie *Sgt. Pepper's Lonely Hearts Club Band*?
9. What set off the worms in *Squirm*?
10. This 1977 documentary about miners striking in Kentucky won an Oscar for Best Documentary. Name it.
11. What was the name of Sherlock Holmes' smarter brother in *The Adventure of Sherlock Holmes' Smarter Brother*, and who played him?
12. What was Roman Polanski's first film after fleeing the U.S.?
13. Who played the part of the imaginary Humphrey Bogart in *Play It Again, Sam*?
14. In *Meteor*, what were Hercules and Peter the Great?
15. What movie did the song "You Light Up My Life" come from?

(answers on page 198)

Gerald Ford

He was Gerald Ford and we weren't. All that really mattered, for a while at least, was that he wasn't Richard Nixon. Ford seemed so nice and normal by comparison. We marveled as he toasted and buttered his own English muffins. Unfortunately, running the country turned out to be a little more difficult.

1. Complete the quote: "I'm a Ford, not a _____."
2. What did "WIN" stand for?
3. Betty Ford said she wouldn't have been surprised if her kids had tried marijuana, but what did Jerry smoke for relaxation?
4. What did Gerald Ford have in common with one of Santa's reindeer?
5. Besides pardoning Richard Nixon, Ford pardoned another notorious badnik. Who? (Clue: It was a woman.)
6. On April 17, 1975, Ford became the first president since Lincoln to do something. What?
7. According to Ford, what was not under Soviet domination?
8. What was unusual about Susan Ford's cat, Shan?

9. President Ford suggested we add a 51st state to the union. What was it?
10. After he became president, Ford had the bust of one of his predecessors installed in the Oval Office. Whose?
11. How did 19-year-old James Salamites and five of his pals get to meet the president in Hartford, Connecticut, in October 1975?
12. Betty Ford offended some people by her response to a question about what she would do if her unmarried daughter were having an affair. Others praised her reaction. What was it?
13. According to *Time* magazine in April 1975, who would Gerald Ford have chosen as his vice president had Nelson Rockefeller turned him down?
14. On Ford's last night in the White House, what did he and Rockefeller whack around?
15. In what 1978 "B" movie did former President Ford make a cameo appearance?

(answers on page 199)

Events 1

Match the event to the year it happened.

1970   a. *Congress approves Panama Canal treaty*
1971   b. *Nixon resigns*
1972   c. *South Vietnam surrenders*
1973   d. *First Earth Day*
1974   e. *Sadat goes to Israel*
1975   f. *Three Mile Island nuclear accident*
1976   g. *Voting age lowered to 18*
1977   h. *Supreme Court legalizes abortion*
1978   i. *Congress passes Equal Rights Amendment*
1979   j. *Bicentennial (duh!)*

(answers on page 200)

Olympics

1. Until the Montreal Olympics, no women from this country had ever won a gold medal in swimming. But at the 1976 games they won 10 of 11 individual titles and broke eight world records. What country were they from?
2. Why did the U.S. basketball team refuse the silver medal at the 1972 games?
3. Who set a world decathlon record at Montreal, with a total of 8,618 points?
4. How many gold medals did Mark Spitz win at the 1972 Olympics, and how many world swimming records did he set?
5. What American swimmer won four gold medals and one silver at the 1976 Olympics, setting world records in the 100-meter and 200-meter backstrokes?
6. Name the West German who, at Innsbruck, became the first woman to win two golds and a silver in Alpine skiing.
7. Where were the 1972 winter Olympics held, and what Dutch skater won three gold medals there?
8. Why was there a 15-bike pileup in one of the bicycling competitions at the Munich games?
9. Who took the gold in women's figure skating at the '76 Olympics?
10. At Montreal, who shattered the world record in the 400-meter hurdles?
11. Why did Rick DeMont, a 16-year-old swimmer from San Rafael, California,

have to give up his gold medal in the 400-meter freestyle at the 1972 games?

12. What four men were on the 1976 U.S. boxing team that won five gold medals?

13. "I fear his career as a sportsman is over," said a Soviet team spokesman in regard to fencer Boris Onischenko, who was whisked back to Kiev during the Montreal Olympics. Why was Boris sent back to the U.S.S.R.?

14. This weightlifter was dubbed the "world's strongest man" after he broke three of his four world records at the 1972 games and then went on to break yet another in Montreal, setting a new record of 561 pounds for the clean and jerk. Who was this superheavyweight?

15. Fourteen years old, five feet tall, and only 86 pounds, she won three gold medals in 1976 and was the first gymnast to score a maximum ten points on the uneven parallel bars. Who was she?

(answers on page 200)

Quotes 3

Who said:

1. "Now we have women marching in the streets! If only things would quiet down!"

    a. *Spiro Agnew*
    b. *Arthur Burns*
    c. *Robert Dole*
    d. *James Kilpatrick*

2. "If it's a woman, it's caustic; if it's a man, it's authoritative. If it's a woman, it's too often pushy; if it's a man, it's aggressive in the best sense of the word."

    a. *Bella Abzug*
    b. *Alan Alda*
    c. *Barbara Walters*
    d. *Miss Piggy*

3. "The claim that American women are downtrodden and unfairly treated is the fraud of the century. The truth is that American women have never had it so good. Why should we lower ourselves to 'equal rights' when we al-

Upon whom is Christian Szell (Laurence Olivier) about to perform some old-fashioned dentistry in *Marathon Man*?

Answer:
Thomas Babington "Babe" Levy (Dustin Hoffman)

ready have the status of special privilege?"

    a. Marabel Morgan
    b. Phyllis Schlafly
    c. Marie Osmond
    d. Renee Richards

4. "Women are not equal and never could be."

    a. Charles Bronson
    b. Telly Savalas
    c. Norman Mailer
    d. Bobby Riggs

5. "I don't consider [the Equal Rights Amendment] a political issue. It is a moral issue.... Where are women mentioned in the Constitution except in the Nineteenth Amendment, giving us the right to vote? When they said all *men* are created equal, they really meant it—otherwise, why did we have to fight for the Nineteenth Amendment?"

    a. Gloria Steinem
    b. Florynce Kennedy

    c. Betty Friedan
    d. Carol Burnett

6. "I support the Equal Rights Amendment because, simply, it's right and necessary."

    a. Leif Garrett
    b. George Foreman
    c. Meatloaf
    d. Howard Cosell

7. "It's one thing to burn your bra and be emancipated, but it's another thing to really feel it. I'm starting to feel respectful of women. I've always liked them but I didn't respect them."

    a. Shirley MacLaine
    b. Jane Fonda
    c. Cher
    d. Englebert Humperdinck

8. "I'm the most liberated woman in the world. Any woman can be liberated if she wants to be. First, she has to convince her husband."

a. *Bo Derek*
b. *Julie Nixon Eisenhower*
c. *June Carter Cash*
d. *Martha Mitchell*

9. "It occurred to me when I was thirteen and wearing white gloves and Mary Janes and going to dancing school, that no one should have to dance backwards all their lives."

    a. *Marlo Thomas*
    b. *Jill Ruckelshaus*
    c. *Erica Jong*
    d. *Twyla Tharp*

10. "When people around you treat you like a child and pay no attention to the things you say, you have to do something."

    a. *Sacheen Littlefeather*
    b. *Johnny Rotten*
    c. *Lynette "Squeaky" Fromme*
    d. *Patty Hearst*

11. "All God's children are not beautiful. Most of God's children are, in fact, barely presentable."

    a. *Woody Allen*
    b. *Erma Bombeck*
    c. *Fran Lebowitz*
    d. *Tammy Faye Bakker*

12. "I was an atheist. Then I became a Christian. Then I became a born-again Christian, and now I have become a Christian patriot. And all that happened in a two-week period."

    a. *Charles Colson*
    b. *Jeb Magruder*
    c. *Eldridge Cleaver*
    d. *Larry Flynt*

13. "We should live our lives as though Christ were coming this afternoon."

    a. *Robert Schuller*
    b. *Jim Bakker*
    c. *Billy Graham*
    d. *Jimmy Carter*

14. "Had I gone my own way and not gotten to know God or accepted Him as a part of my life, I think that I would have been a very belligerent individual, full of hate and bitterness."

    a. *Jimmy Swaggart*
    b. *Pat Robertson*
    c. *Jerry Falwell*
    d. *Anita Bryant*

15. "Why is it when we talk to God, we're said to be praying—but when God talks to us, we're schizophrenic?"

    a. *Maharaj Ji*
    b. *Jim Jones*
    c. *Sun Myung Moon*
    d. *Lily Tomlin*

(answers on page 201)

TV 6

1. Name the variety program hosted by a pair of mimes.
2. What was the real name of the Fonz?
3. Who was the first bandleader on *Saturday Night Live*?
4. What was Fluffy prime minister of?
5. Cheryl Stoppelmoor was a regular on *The Ken Berry "Wow" Show* in the early '70s. By the late '70s she was famous under another name in one of the premier "jiggle shows" of the decade. What was the program, and what name was she using by then?
6. Whom did Howard Borden live next door to?
7. *Tabitha* may have been a witch, but she also had a job in the mortal world. What was it?
8. Who was Sam, of *Sam*?
9. What was *Police Woman* "Pepper" Anderson's first name?
10. Who were the original Sweathogs?
11. When Mary Richards was jailed for refusing to reveal a source on *The Mary Tyler Moore Show*, what was the only thing she brought to jail with her?
12. Why did Esther Rolle quit *Good Times* in 1977?
13. Who was Quincy's assistant on *Quincy, M.E.*?
14. In 1971 Captain Kangaroo visited Mister Rogers on his TV show. Then, a few weeks later, Mister Rogers visited Captain Kangaroo on his program. Why?
15. Who played Chet Kinkaid?

(answers on page 201)

Endorsements

Match the celebrity to the product he or she endorsed.

1. Chrysler
2. Mr. Coffee
3. Fruit of the Loom
4. d-Con Roach Killer
5. Ultra-Brite
6. Wella Balsam
7. Alka-Seltzer
8. Serta
9. Polaroid
10. Excedrin
11. Coffee-mate
12. Volkswagen
13. Teacher's Scotch
14. La-Z-Boy
15. Kodak Instamatic
16. Hamilton-Beach Popcorn Popper
17. Lipton Cup O'Noodles
18. Hertz
19. Kleenex
20. Mr. Coffee

a. *Sammy Davis, Jr.*
b. *Joanne Worley*
c. *Steve Allen and Jayne Meadows*
d. *JoJo Starbuck*
e. *Reggie Jackson*
f. *Susan Anton*
g. *Neil Armstrong*
h. *Farrah Fawcett-Majors*
i. *Joe Namath*
j. *Mel Brooks*
k. *Howard Cosell*
l. *Farrah Fawcett-Majors*
m. *David Janssen*
n. *James Garner*
o. *O. J. Simpson*
p. *Joe Namath*
q. *Muhammad Ali*
r. *Cybil Shepherd*
s. *Joe Dimaggio*
t. *Joe Garagiola*

(answers on page 202)

What kind of melons did *Mr. Majestyk* (Charles Bronson) grow?

Women 3

1. In 1974, even though Kathryn Kirschbaum was mayor of Davenport, Iowa, and earned $15,000 a year (a respectable sum for that time), she was unable to get a BankAmericard unless she did what?

2. When asked his opinion of the ERA, Arizona Governor Jack Williams said he "hadn't finished reading it yet." It was only 24 words long. Can you recite it?

3. What was pronounced a certifiable psychiatric illness, according to the American Psychiatric Association in 1976?

4. Why did 30 women deposit a box of baby chicks on the desk of the manager of a Boston radio station in 1970?

5. What was the Women's Strike for Equality, and on what anniversary did it occur?

6. And what was National Celebration of Womanhood Day?

7. Who were Anna Fisher, Shannon Lucid, Judith Resnik, Sally Ride, Margaret Seddon, and Kathryn Sullivan?

8. What happened at *Newsweek* magazine shortly after its cover story "Women in Revolt" came out in 1970?

9. What made Frances "Sissy" Farenthold famous in 1972?

10. *The Washington Post* changed its classified ad section in 1972. How?

11. Why did Sarah Caldwell become the first woman to conduct at the Metropolitan Opera in 1976?

12. What did NOW want *Sesame Street* to do during its second season?

13. In 1979 two women became leaders of their respective countries: Pakistan and Great Britain. Name these women.

14. What was notable about Rosaura Jiminez's death in 1977?

15. In 1974 Joan Little, a 20-year-old black prisoner in the Beaufort County, North Carolina, jail, stabbed her white jailer, Clarence Alligood, 11 times with an ice pick that he kept in his desk drawer. She was charged with first-degree murder but was found not guilty. Why?

(answers on page 202)

Numbers—Politics

Match the correct number to each item.

1. As of the mid-'70s, the percentage of Britons polled who thought Queen Elizabeth II had been chosen by God to rule
2. By 1976, the percentage of U.S. voters who would consider voting for a woman presidential candidate
3. The percentage by which George McGovern said he stood behind running mate Tom Eagleton in 1972
4. The percentage of the vote received by George McGovern in 1972
5. The number of impeachment counts voted against Richard Nixon by the House Judiciary Committee
6. The percentage of Americans polled in August 1973 who said they would vote for McGovern over Nixon if the 1972 election were held over
7. The number of words per minute Elizabeth Ray could type, according to fellow congressional office workers
8. The number of states carried by Gerald Ford in the 1976 election
9. The number of electoral votes received by Ronald Reagan in 1976
10. The number of portable plastic toilets erected in downtown Plains, Georgia, to accommodate tourists following Jimmy Carter's 1976 election victory

    a. 1,000
    b. 1
    c. 51
    d. 33
    e. 3
    f. 12
    g. 10
    h. 27
    i. 73
    j. 38

(answers on page 203)

Music 3

1. The Partridge Family had three top-ten hits, which was particularly impressive since they didn't even know how to play their own instruments. Name the songs.
2. David Cassidy's little brother, Shaun, had his first big hit in 1977, also on a TV

series. What was the hit, and what was the series?

3. Who was Ginger Alden?

4. The '60s had Woodstock. What was the biggest rock festival of the '70s?

5. Who held his first all-gospel concert on November 1, 1979?

6. Harry Wayne Casey and Richard Finch organized this group in 1975 and immediately hit the charts with "Get Down Tonight" and "That's the Way (I Like It)." What was the group?

7. When Eric Clapton married George Harrison's ex-wife, Patti, on May 19, 1979, three of the former Beatles played at their wedding. Who didn't?

8. This guy was named the Country Music Association's Male Vocalist of the Year three times during the '70s—more than anyone else. Who?

9. Who was Scooter Herring, and why was he sentenced to 75 years in jail?

10. "Disco Lady" was the first single ever to be certified platinum, selling more than two million copies in 1976. Who sang it?

11. In 1978 Soviet police were unable to control 4,000 frenzied fans who had come to see what rock star in Leningrad?

12. Who was Daryl Dragon?

13. This country band poked fun at its ethnic background in such songs as "Ride 'em, Jewboy" and "They Ain't Makin' Jews Like Jesus Anymore." Name the band.

14. The "Another Somebody Done Somebody Wrong Song" was a hit for not one, not two, but three different acts. Name 'em.

15. What symphony conductor in 1970 offered to take drugs as part of a test to determine their effect on the performance and enjoyment of music?

(answers on page 204)

TV Expressions

Name the TV character responsible for each of the popular expressions below.

1. Who loves ya, baby?
2. Aaayyh
3. Lookin' good
4. Dy-no-mite
5. What you see is what you get

6. Kiss my grits
7. Book 'em, Dan-o
8. Never mind
9. Dat's da name o' dat tune
10. There you go
11. Shazbat
12. I'm coming, Elizabeth, I'm coming
13. Stifle yourself
14. But no-o-o-o-o-o
15. It's always something
16. Sit on it
17. Da plane, da plane
18. The Devil made me do it
19. You can take dat to da bank
20. It all started at a 5,000-watt radio station in Fresno, California

(answers on page 204)

Movies 6

1. What was 25 feet long, weighed one ton, was made of polyurethane and neoprene foam over steel—and was named Bruce?
2. In *A Clockwork Orange*, who was Alex's (Malcolm McDowell's) favorite composer?
3. What documentary featured Arnold Schwarzenegger and Lou Ferrigno participating in a Mr. Olympia contest held in Pretoria, South Africa?
4. In *A Boy and His Dog*, what was the name of the dog, and who played him?
5. What two words did Eddie (Meatloaf) have written on his fingers in *The Rocky Horror Picture Show*?
6. Who wanted disc jockey Dave Garland (Clint Eastwood) to "Play 'Misty' for me"?
7. In what film did Carrie Fisher make her screen debut?
8. In *Invasion of the Bee Girls*, how were the male scientists dying?
9. *Chinatown* director Roman Polanski had a small part in the movie. As whom?
10. *Marco*, a musical based on the travels of Marco Polo, starred Zero Mostel as Kublai Khan. Who played Marco Polo?
11. In Werner Herzog's film *Aguirre: The Wrath of God*, what were the conquistadors looking for?
12. This 1976 film, starring Elizabeth Taylor, Jane Fonda, Cicely Tyson, and Ava Gardner, was the first Russian-American co-production. Name it.

Randle Patrick McMurphy (Jack Nicholson) is trying to shoot some hoops with whom?

Answer:
Chief Bromden (Will Sampson), in One Flew Over the Cuckoo's Nest

13. What was the 1970 sequel to the X-rated Swedish film *I Am Curious (Yellow)*?
14. The entire cast of this 1972 movie consisted of Laurence Olivier and Michael Caine. Name it.
15. In *American Graffiti*, what was the name of the gang that Curt Henderson (Richard Dreyfuss) rode around with and was asked to join?

(answers on page 206)

Trends 2

1. In 1975 California advertising executive Gary Dahl bought 2½ tons of rocks from a Mexican beach and did what with them?
2. The last assembly-line convertible built in the U.S. rolled out of the factory on April 22, 1976. What make of car was it?
3. Name the law firm that, in 1977, became the first to advertise on TV.
4. In 1978 the first postage stamp in honor of a black woman was issued. Whose face was on it?
5. This stun gun, developed for law enforcement, could deliver a 50,000-volt charge. In 1975 it became quite popular with private citizens, including criminals. What was it called?
6. In the mid-'70s you could get an AMC Gremlin or a Zenith color television decorated with what fashionable material?
7. These ranged from 2 to 5 inches in height and attracted the attention of fashion-conscious young men in 1972. What were they?
8. Who was on the cover of *People*'s premiere issue on March 4, 1974?
9. These hit men were available for about $35 and for a brief time in the mid-'70s creamed hundreds of people from coast to coast. With what weapon?
10. After nearly a century of classifying this condition as a mental illness, the American Psychiatric Association changed its mind in 1973 and declared that it "does not meet the criteria for being a psychiatric disorder." What was it?
11. What was the purpose of the organization "Call Off Your Old Tired Ethics," formed in 1973?

12. In 1979 Wesley and Helen LaRoya settled in for a nice evening at a favorite
'70s pastime, during which they fell
asleep and died. What was it?
13. This 35,000-year-old supernatural being first "appeared" in Washington
state in 1978 and later went on *The
Merv Griffin Show*. Who was he?
14. In 1979 a Jehovah's Witness refused a
needed blood transfusion on religious
grounds but survived anyway. How?
15. What change in church rules did God
suggest to Mormon President Spencer
W. Kimball in 1978?

(answers on page 205)

First Lines 2

Match the first line with the book it came
from.

1. "Call me Smitty."
2. "Mira was hiding in the ladies' room."
3. "In Beverly Hills only the infirm and the
senile do not drive their own cars."
4. "'Listen to me.'"
5. "Jack Torrance thought: *Officious little
prick.*"
6. "The blaze of the sun wrung pops of
sweat from the old man's brow, yet he
cupped his hands around the glass of
hot sweet tea as if to warm them."
7. "They didn't say anything about this in
the books, I thought, as the snow blew
in through the gaping doorway and
settled on my naked back."
8. "The truth is, if old Major Dover hadn't
dropped dead at Taunton races Jim
would never have come to Thursgood's
at all."
9. "In 1902 Father built a house at the
crest of the Broadview Avenue hill in
New Rochelle, New York."
10. "The road to perfect sex begins with a
perfect you."
11. "I planned my death carefully; unlike
my life, which meandered along from
one thing to another, despite my feeble
attempts to control it."
12. "Much of the American wealth is an il-
lusion which is being secretly gnawed
away and much of it will be completely
wiped out in the near future."
13. "I had always lied to my mother."

14. "Every time he drove through Yorkville, Rosenbaum got angry, just on general principles."
15. "This is a book about what happens to people when they are overwhelmed by change."

    a. Fools Die *by Mario Puzo*
    b. Lady Oracle *by Margaret Atwood*
    c. Tinker, Tailor, Soldier, Spy *by John le Carré*
    d. The Exorcist *by William Peter Blatty*
    e. The Great American Novel *by Philip Roth*
    f. The Dieter's Guide to Weight Loss During Sex *by Richard Smith*
    g. My Mother/My Self *by Nancy Friday*
    h. Future Shock *by Alvin Toffler*
    i. The Women's Room *by Marilyn French*
    j. The Shining *by Stephen King*
    k. How to Prosper During the Coming Bad Years *by Howard J. Ruff*
    l. All Creatures Great and Small *by James Herriot*
    m. Scruples *by Judith Krantz*
    n. Marathon Man *by William Goldman*
    o. Ragtime *by E. L. Doctorow*

(answers on page 206)

Sports 2

1. What team owner said, in 1973, "I won't be active in the day-to-day operation of the club at all. I've spread myself so thin. I've got enough headaches with my shipbuilding company."
2. What two people was Billy Martin talking about when he said, in 1978, "They deserve each other. One's a born liar; the other's convicted."
3. What was *Double Eagle II*?
4. Why did Georgia Governor Lester Maddox declare October 26, 1970, a day of mourning in his state?
5. Name the 21-year-old golfer who, in 1978, won nine tournaments and became golf's all-time rookie money winner.

6. This three-year-old filly had tied or broken records in eight of her 10 starts and was leading in a 1975 match race with Kentucky Derby winner Foolish Pleasure when the bones in her foreleg snapped. What was her name?

7. In 1976 Baltimore Colts quarterback Bert Jones threatened to leave the team if owner Robert Irsay did not rehire whom?

8. With what World Football League team did Larry Csonka, Jim Kiick, and Paul Warfield of the NFL champion Miami Dolphins sign on March 31, 1974?

9. Until 1975 they had not won a World Series in 35 years. In '76, however, they won their second in a row, sweeping the Yankees in four games. Who were they?

10. And who was their National League MVP in 1976, for the second year in a row?

11. Name the horse that won the Triple Crown in 1978 and name the jockey who rode it, the youngest jockey ever to ride a Triple Crown winner.

12. What annual 1,200-mile dog sled race was started in 1973 and took the winner 20 days to complete?

13. What team set the NBA record in the '70s for the most losses during a season?

14. In 1978 Victor Korchnoi claimed his Soviet opponent in the world chess championship was using a parapsychologist in the audience to psych him out. Who was the opponent, and who won the title?

15. Name the skipper of the yacht *Courageous*, which successfully defended the America's Cup from Australian challengers in 1977.

(answers on page 206)

TV 7

1. What gave *Wonder Woman* her powers?

2. What TV character's decision to have an abortion led CBS to grant free airtime to the U.S. Catholic Conference in 1973 to state their antiabortion views?

3. Whom did Alice Nelson work for?

4. Although this show's first three seasons featured a woman with two children and a large dog, at the start of the

show's fourth and final year she was suddenly single with no kids, no dog, and no explanation for what had happened. Name the show.

5. Who was Elliot Carlin?

6. What was *Kojak*'s first name?

7. Who was the only actor to star in both the movie and TV show *M*A*S*H*, and what character did he play?

8. Where did Richie, Potsie, and Ralph go to college?

9. This show was based on the works of James Thurber and used Thurber-like cartoons to animate its hero's dreams and fears. Name it.

10. Who was Frank "Ponch" Poncherello's partner on *C.H.i.P.s*?

11. What was the name of the barbershop that Clifton Curtis ran on *That's My Mama*?

12. Who was Peggy Fair?

13. Steve Austin was *The Six Million Dollar Man*. A backup for him was built, however—a *seven*-million dollar man. What was *his* name?

14. Name the Western in which the lead character (played by James Garner) was shot and killed so that his more traditionally heroic twin brother (again played by James Garner) could become the star and improve ratings.

15. This show, featuring Tom Snyder, broke TV's final frontier: very late night. It didn't start until 1 A.M. Name it.

(answers on page 207)

Quotes—True Or False?

Nine of the following ten quotes are real. Which one is fiction?

1. Director George Lucas, on the success of *Star Wars:* "It just has to do with people liking dumb movies."

2. H. R. Haldeman, on how to avoid a Watergate subpoena: "We move to Camp David and hide. They can't get in there."

3. Michael Jackson, explaining why he turned down the part of the gay dancer in the film version of *A Chorus Line:* "People already think I'm that way—homo—because of my voice, and I'm not."

4. Peter Finch, on how he could bring himself to kiss a man onscreen in *Sun-*

day, *Bloody Sunday:* "I just closed my eyes and thought of England."

5. Pat Nixon, when asked in 1978 what course of life she would take if she were young and starting out again: "Well, I recently tried disco dancing to the radio. I would dance more."

6. Pope John Paul I, shortly after being elected pope: "If someone had told me I would be pope one day, I would have studied harder."

7. Jimmy Carter, when asked how he would feel if his daughter told him she were having an affair: "Shocked and overwhelmed. My daughter is seven years old."

8. John Mitchell, upon hearing of *The Washington Post's* Watergate investigation: "Katie Graham's gonna get her tit caught in a big fat wringer."

9. Maharaj Ji, after being asked by a reporter, "Are you the son of God?" "Everybody's the son of God. You ain't the uncle or aunt of God, are you?"

10. Director Tom Laughlin, when asked if he'd make yet another *Billy Jack* movie: "As long as there's still madness running this country, as long as people are rummaging in garbage cans for food,

you're goddamned right we'll make another one!"

(answer on page 207)

Movies 7

1. What planet was Dr. Frank N. Furter from in *The Rocky Horror Picture Show*?

2. A young Sylvester Stallone (pre-*Rocky*) and Henry Winkler (pre-*Happy Days*) starred in this 1974 movie about young New York hoods. Name it.

3. The theme song went, "Who's the black private dick that's a sex machine to all the chicks?" OK, so who was he?

4. How much did Marlon Brando receive for his 12 days of work portraying Superman's father, Jor-El, in *Superman*?

5. The movie *C.H.O.M.P.S.* was about a mechanical dog. What did C.H.O.M.P.S. stand for?

6. Name the musical that was a spoof of Prohibition-era gangster films and featured children in all the roles.

7. What violent 1971 cop movie did a local Philippine police department re-

See Jane. See Jane look terrified. Why was Jane afraid?

Answer:
She feared that the nuclear power plant she was visiting was seriously on the fritz, in The China Syndrome

quest a copy of to use as a training film?

8. Truman Capote made his screen debut as an actor in this movie. Name it.
9. What took place at the Kit Kat Klub?
10. Name the 1972 Brian DePalma film, starring Tommy Smothers and Orson Welles, about a man who left his establishment job to become a tap-dancing magician.
11. What was the full title of the Lina Wertmuller movie *Swept Away*?
12. Name the 1976 movie based on a 1967 hit song by Bobbie Gentry.
13. Name the 1978 movie based on a 1968 hit song by Jeannie C. Riley.
14. Who said to Cindy Sondheim (Susan St. James)—and he should know—"In a world without romance, it is better to be dead"?
15. Hard to believe, but there were three *Bad News Bears* films during the '70s. Name them.

(answers on page 207)

Which Came First?

It was the decade that gave us Mood Rings and nuclear-powered pacemakers, windup plastic Jimmy Carter peanuts and fern bars. Do you remember which came first?

1. VHS or Betamax?
2. The video game or the space shuttle?
3. Garfield or Heathcliff?
4. The disappearance of Jimmy Hoffa or legalized gambling in Atlantic City?
5. The Moral Majority or the first rabies vaccine?
6. The demise of *Life* or the demise of *Look*?
7. The revival of *Life* or the revival of *Look*?
8. Genetic engineering or the first female-to-male transsexual operation?
9. Lite beer or the arrival of Perrier in the U.S.?
10. Heritage U.S.A. or Disney World?
11. Sears Tower or the World Trade Center?
12. The first home computer or Rubik's Cube?

13. The Sony Walkman or the compact disc?
14. The Cuisinart or the Heimlich maneuver?
15. Airline baggage safety checks or the discovery of the first black hole?

(answers on page 208)

Music 4

1. In January 1972, two guys were kicked off the stage at the Hollywood Palladium for attempting to jam with Chuck Berry. Berry later apologized to them, saying he didn't know who they were. Who were they?
2. After many long nights studying the works of Carlos Castaneda with the help of peyote and raw tequila, this group decided to name itself after a major figure in the Native American cosmos. What name did they decide upon?
3. Who said, "I gave up rock 'n' roll for the Rock of Ages"?
4. This group performed their revival of the 1962 dance hit "The Loco-Motion" in front of a giant screen showing film footage of a train crash. Name the group.
5. Who made her movie debut as the Acid Queen in *Tommy*?
6. Name the Osmonds, or at least the seven who regularly appeared on the family TV show. What was their only No. 1 song as a group?
7. Jazz guitar wiz John McLaughlin became a disciple of the Indian guru Sri Chinmoy and formed a band, which he named what?
8. "Now you got your dead cat and you got your dead dog/On a moonlight night you got your dead toad frog," sang Loudon Wainwright III in 1973. What else you got?
9. Fleetwood Mac's *Rumours* was put together at the same time as two couples in the band were falling apart. Who were the couples?
10. Better known as a comedian, this star had a hit song in 1973 entitled "The Night the Lights Went Out in Georgia." Who was she?

11. What moved from Detroit to L.A. in 1972?
12. Eleven people were trampled to death as rock fans rushed the gates at a 1979 concert. Where did it happen, and what group was playing?
13. What conductor caused a stir by playing the music of Richard Wagner, a composer considered by many to be anti-Semitic, in Israel?
14. In March 1975, all six of this group's albums were on the *Billboard* chart at the same time. Who were they?
15. Who was on the cover of *Beat* for 37 consecutive months in the early '70s, during which time millions of girls went through puberty?

(answers on page 209)

Those Wonderful Nixon Years

1. What was Operation Gemstone?
2. Who discovered the open door that led to the arrest of the Watergate burglars and the eventual resignation of a president?

3. Who took credit for the famous 18½-minute gap during a tape of a pivotal conversation between Nixon and H. R. Haldeman?
4. Fill in the bumper sticker lines:

    a. *Jail to the* _____
    b. *Impeachment with* _____
    c. *Don't blame me, I'm from* _____

5. Who was Alexander Butterfield?
6. Who said she was interrupted during a June 1972 phone conversation with UPI reporter Helen Thomas, then thrown to the floor and stuck with a hypodermic needle, after which the phone was ripped from the wall—all this by a man who would later become head of security for the Committee to Reelect the President?
7. Who was found dead in a plane crash with $10,000 in "hush money" in her purse?
8. Fill in the blanks:

    During the Saturday Night Massacre on October 20, 1973, President Nixon wanted Attorney General (a) _____ to fire Watergate special prosecutor (b) _____. The prosecutor, it seems, had been trying to obtain some tape recordings of Oval Office conversations. The attorney general refused and resigned and was replaced by the deputy attorney general, (c) _____. He also refused to carry out Nixon's order and was fired. Finally, the solicitor general, (d) _____, who would become slightly better known for other reasons in the 1980s, agreed to Nixon's request.

9. Mark items a–f true or false:

During the 1972 Democratic primaries, White House dirty tricksters put out fake campaign literature under the name of presidential candidate Edmund Muskie that:

    a. *stated that Muskie opponent Henry M. Jackson had fathered a child out of wedlock*
    b. *stated that Jackson had been arrested on charges of homosexuality—twice*
    c. *stated that Muskie opponent Hubert Humphrey had been arrested on drunken-driving charges*
    d. *stated that Humphrey had been in the company of a call girl at the time*
    e. *stated that Muskie opponent George McGovern had forged $2,000 in checks as a young man*
    f. *stated that he had done so to help pay for the illegal abortion of a child he had fathered out of wedlock*

10. Name the man responsible for the lies above.

(answers on page 209)

Blaxploitation Movies

Fifteen of the following are real titles of '70s blaxploitation movies; five are fake. Can you tell which is which?

Blacula
Scream, Blacula, Scream
Blackenstein
The Blaxorcist
Dr. Black and Mr. Hyde
Blackasaurus
Blackasaurus vs. Honkeytown
Super Dude
Superfly T.N.T.
T.N.T. Jackson
Afrodisiac Jones
Pantherella
Black Eye
Black Fist
Black Caesar
Black Godfather
Black Shampoo
Black Samson
Black Jesus
Black Bikers from Hell

(answers on page 210)

Journalism

1. What taboo was broken by the National Press Club in 1971?
2. What TV news show began its run as an ongoing special report called *America Held Hostage*?
3. Who fathered "gonzo" journalism?
4. Why did California's tiny *Point Reyes Light* win a Pulitzer Prize in 1979?
5. On the cover of what magazine did Hamilton Jordan and Jody Powell appear dressed as a vaudeville team?
6. Who was "Woodstein"?
7. Who was Deep Throat?
8. Who was Don Bolles and what were his last words?
9. What magazine, written and edited by women, began publication in 1972?
10. This 1971 CBS documentary hosted by Roger Mudd created such a stir that a House subcommittee wanted to cite the network for contempt for refusing to disclose background material. Vice President Agnew called the program "disreputable," so CBS must have been doing something right. What was the program?

11. Why did *Time* magazine's Man of the Year for 1979 lead to a number of cancelled subscriptions?
12. In 1976 she became the first woman to co-anchor an evening news show, for which she was reportedly paid $1 million. Her lesser-paid co-anchor, however, was not happy. Who were they and what network were they on?
13. What journalist served as the intermediary, via a satellite link, between Anwar Sadat and Menachem Begin, during which Sadat said he would go to Israel and Begin said Israel would welcome him?
14. Name the ABC correspondent executed by members of Anastasio Somoza's Nicaraguan National Guard in 1979.
15. Why did former Detroit newsman Jerald terHorst resign as White House press secretary in 1974?

(answers on page 210)

Women 4

1. In 1974 little girls were able to do something that they had never been allowed to do before. What?
2. Who was John Rideout's wife, and why did she take him to court?
3. What was "Alice Doesn't!" day?
4. When Fay Wattleton was elected president of Planned Parenthood in 1978, she was the first black to hold that post. There was another first about her election, too. What?
5. First introduced in 1923, the Equal Rights Amendment finally received Senate passage in 1973. Which state was the first to ratify it?
6. And how long after the ERA had been sent to the states did it take this state to vote for ratification?
7. Why did NOW denounce Mattel's "Growing Up Skipper" doll in 1975?
8. Who said, at the Grammy Awards in 1972, "I want to thank . . . God because She makes everything possible"?
9. In 1971 women finally won the right to vote in what European country?
10. What happened to the National Association for Repeal of Abortion Laws

Who was this man, and where was he trying to go? (And, no, "the Ponderosa" is not an acceptable answer.)

Answer:
Lorne Greene played Captain Adama of Battlestar Galactica, which was trying to find its way home to Earth.

after *Roe* v. *Wade* legalized most abortions?

11. In 1979 six female Directors Guild of America members went through guild records to determine how many movies had been made by women during the past 30 years. Of the 7,332 feature films released from 1949 to 1979, how many did they find that had been directed by women?

12. What did women have to practically beg to do in Louisiana until 1975?

13. Name the woman who sought the 1976 Democratic presidential nomination on an antiabortion platform.

14. This former soprano became the first female general director of the New York City Opera in 1979. Name her.

15. Until the mid-'70s, the only way a woman had ever been elected governor was by following her husband into office. That changed in 1974, however, when this woman was elected governor of Connecticut in her own right. Name her.

(answers on page 211)

Numbers—Sports

Match the correct number to each item.

1. The record number of touchdowns scored by O. J. Simpson in 1975

2. The record number of bases stolen by Lou Brock in 1974

3. The amount, in thousands, that constituted baseball's minimum salary in 1976

4. The number of dollars, in millions, amassed by Muhammad Ali as of August 1978

5. In minutes, the total penalties assessed against the Philadelphia Flyers in 1975–6

6. The amount per floor, in pennies, that George Willig was fined for illegally climbing the outside of the 115-story World Trade Center

7. The percentage of the shoe sales market held by running shoes as of 1978

8. The bonus, in dollars, offered to Oakland A's ballplayers by owner Charlie O. Finley for growing a moustache for a special Moustache Night promotion in 1972

9. The number of the 25 players who grew moustaches

10. The amount, in thousands, that Schick offered Mark Spitz to shave off his moustache

    a. 56
    b. 300
    c. 1,980
    d. 23
    e. 118
    f. 50
    g. 16.5
    h. 25
    i. 19
    j. 1

(answers on page 212)

TV 8

1. A revival of *The Brady Bunch* was attempted in the late '70s. Called *The Brady Bunch Hour*, this program lasted only five months. All but one of *The Brady Bunch* cast members returned. Who didn't, and who took his/her place?
2. What did the "O" in *Harry-O* stand for?
3. Who hailed from Crabapple Cove, Maine?
4. Why did Carol Burnett tug on her ear at the end of each episode of *The Carol Burnett Show*?
5. This show won three Emmys for Best Dramatic Series during the '70s, more than any other program. Name it.
6. Who was "The Happy Homemaker"?
7. What was the name of Tom and Eddie Corbett's housekeeper on *The Court-ship of Eddie's Father*?
8. Two shows during the '70s had as their heroes invisible people. Name the shows.
9. Who was Reuben Kinkaid?
10. What defiant act did Miss Jane Pittman perform at the end of *The Autobiography of Miss Jane Pittman*?
11. Name the program that featured a blind insurance-company investigator. What was his guide dog's name?
12. Who were Pete Malloy and Jim Reed?
13. These performers tired of Los Angeles and so built a $2.5 million studio in Orem, Utah, where they taped their shows. Who were they?
14. What was *Ironside's* first name?

What high school did the criminal element above attend, and in what police precinct did they find themselves here?

Answer:
James Buchanan High School; the 12th Precinct. The Sweathogs from Welcome Back, Kotter were featured on an episode of Barney Miller.

15. This comedy writer, who later went on to host his own talk show, was a regular in comedy sketches on *The Starland Vocal Band Show* and *Mary*. Name him.

(answers on page 212)

People 4

1. Lazlo Toth screamed, "I am Jesus Christ!" while battering this famous statue with a hammer. What statue?
2. This model appeared in a *Sports Illustrated* swimsuit edition facing the camera in a transparent white fishnet bathing suit. Her wet suit clearly showed her breasts, nipples and all. Name her.
3. What secretary of agriculture was forced to resign after telling a racist joke?
4. Who was the Son of Sam? For that matter, who was Sam?
5. In 1971 Jane Fonda, Donald Sutherland, and other actors made a tour of GI coffeehouses with an alternative to Bob Hope's official show. They called their satirical antiwar revue *FTA*. What did *FTA* stand for?
6. Karol Wojtyla became Pope John Paul II. What was the name of the man who had been Pope John Paul I?
7. Why did the U.S. Fish and Wildlife Service file two misdemeanor charges against Dr. Sherman Thomas after he "birdied" the 17th hole of the Congressional Country Club in Bethesda, Maryland, on May 3, 1979?
8. Leslie King, Jr., and Elizabeth Bloomer became famous in the '70s. By what names were they better known?
9. For what did Soviet defector Arkady Shevchenko allegedly pay $5,000 a month in CIA money, which taxpayers in 1978 thought was a poor use of funds?
10. This leader, a great believer in the occult, once tried to protect Phnom Penh from attack by sending a wizard up in a helicopter to sprinkle a ring of magic sand around the city. Name him.
11. Who became the first member of Great Britain's immediate royal family to get a divorce since King Henry VIII divorced Anne of Cleves in 1540?

12. This transvestite actor starred in such cult classics as *Pink Flamingos* and *Female Trouble*. His birth name was Harris Glenn Milstead, but by what name was she better known?

13. Nineteen-year-old Saudi Princess Misha'il was publicly executed in July 1977. Smuggled film footage of her execution was later shown on European and American TV as *Death of a Princess*, despite Saudi protests and efforts to keep it off the air. For what crime was this young woman executed?

14. Which U.S. Supreme Court justice did Representative Gerald Ford move to impeach in 1970?

15. This UCLA basketball coach had guided his team to an unprecedented 10 national championships in 12 years by the time he retired in 1975. Name him.

(answers on page 212)

First Lines 3

Match the first line with the book it came from.

1. "Where to begin?"
2. "I get the willies when I see closed doors."
3. "After the children's nap, I repeated the morning's chores in an abbreviated fashion."
4. "I was born in the house my father built."
5. "Commander Victor Henry rode a taxicab home from the Navy Building on Constitution Avenue, in a gusty gray March rainstorm that matched his mood."
6. "A screaming comes across the sky."
7. "In trying to solve the terrifying problems that face us in the world today, we naturally turn to the things we do best."
8. "Premeditated crime: the longer the meditation, the dreaming, the more triumphant the execution!"
9. "I felt like the walking wounded as I mounted the stairs and opened the

door of the second-floor apartment I had rented only that morning."

10. "Who is there who has not felt a sudden startled pang at reliving an old experience or feeling an old emotion?"

11. "Brenda was six when she fell out of the apple tree."

12. "One gray November morning I was running along the edge of a lake in Winchester, Massachusetts, a suburb north of Boston."

13. "He did not expect to see blood."

14. "Sandy sat up in bed and looked at the clock."

15. "Within five minutes, or ten minutes, no more than that, three of the others had called her on the telephone to ask her if she had heard that something had happened out there."

    a. Wifey *by Judy Blume*
    b. Curtain *by Agatha Christie*
    c. Gravity's Rainbow *by Thomas Pynchon*
    d. Kalki *by Gore Vidal*
    e. Beyond Freedom and Dignity *by B. F. Skinner*
    f. Kramer vs. Kramer *by Avery Corman*

    g. Up the Sandbox! *by Anne Richardson Roiphe*
    h. The Executioner's Song *by Norman Mailer*
    i. RN: The Memoirs of Richard Nixon *by Richard Nixon*
    j. Something Happened *by Joseph Heller*
    k. The Right Stuff *by Tom Wolfe*
    l. Do With Me What You Will *by Joyce Carol Oates*
    m. The Winds of War *by Herman Wouk*
    n. Creative Divorce *by Mel Krantzler*
    o. The Complete Book of Running *by James F. Fixx*

(answers on page 214)

Movies 8

1. Where did Harold (Bud Cort) and Maude (Ruth Gordon) meet?
2. In *Star Wars*, what was Princess Leia's (Carrie Fisher's) last name?
3. After the popularity of the boxing movie *Rocky*, Hollywood thought that the world was ready for the story of a boxing kangaroo. They were wrong; the film bombed. Name the kangaroo.
4. What song did Dr. Frankenstein (Gene Wilder) and the monster (Peter Boyle) sing and dance to in *Young Frankenstein*?
5. In the '70s, what was Rosebud?
6. Roger Moore first starred as James Bond in what film?
7. Who were Ben and Socrates?
8. Farrah Fawcett made her screen debut in a film that featured her in a lesbian love scene with Raquel Welch. Name the film.
9. Aboard what space station did Lowell (Bruce Dern) tend to the last samples of Earth's vegetation in *Silent Running*?
10. Who played Dick and Jane, and what was their idea of fun?
11. What team did Phil Elliott (Nick Nolte) play for in *North Dallas 40*?
12. In *The End*, Sonny Lawson (Burt Reynolds) was dying of a toxic blood disease. He didn't tell his daughter he was dying, however. What did he tell her was happening to him?
13. This 1974 *Bonnie and Clyde* knockoff is mostly notable for showing Angie Dickinson and William Shatner in nude encounters. Name it.
14. What was the name of Quint's (Robert Shaw's) boat in *Jaws*?
15. Name the real-life sportscaster who gave the play-by-play of Fielding (Woody Allen) and Nancy's (Louise Lasser's) wedding night in *Bananas*.

(answers on page 214)

TV Detectives

The '70s saw a crime wave on TV, and no, we're not talking about *Hee Haw Honeys* and other programs that were so bad it should have been a felony to air them. We're talking about TV cop and detective shows. Some characters from these shows became so popular, in fact, that their names were better known than those of the actors who played them. Who portrayed the crime-fighters below?

1. Columbo
2. Kojak
3. Cannon
4. Jim Rockford
5. Ironside
6. Barnaby Jones
7. Baretta
8. McCloud
9. Harry-O
10. Stewart McMillan
11. Dan August
12. Mannix
13. Quincy
14. Banacek
15. Hec Ramsey

(answers on page 215)

Music 5

1. It was *Star Wars* meets rock star during this 1977 concert tour. Who performed onstage with a replica of R2-D2?
2. What was Michael Jackson's first solo recording to reach the top of the charts?
3. What New Wave group sang, "This ain't no party. This ain't no disco. This ain't no foolin' around"?
4. In what year did the Beatles break up?
5. The Sugar Hill Gang cut the first rap record in 1979. Based on a track from Chic's "Good Times," it established rap's basic sound. What was the song called?
6. During the '70s, two No. 1 hits came from TV shows, one in 1975 and the other in 1976. What were they?
7. This Academy Award–winning composer filed for bankruptcy in 1976 with debts of $6 million resulting from failed business ventures. Among them was a fast-food chain called Hot Buttered Soul Ltd. Who was he?
8. What Leonard Bernstein work was commissioned for the opening of the Kennedy Center in 1971?
9. Who, in 1972, became the first woman to win the Country Music Association's Entertainer of the Year award?
10. In 1974 this singer's ex-girlfriend attacked him with boiling grits while he was showering and then shot herself to

death, an incident credited with intensifying his shift from sexy songs to gospel sounds. Who was he?

11. Who was found dead in a Paris bathtub in July 1971?

12. With whom did John Lennon make his last onstage appearance?

13. Who played Franz Liszt in Ken Russell's 1975 flop, *Lisztomania*?

14. Which two tennis stars was Paul Anka writing about in "I Believe There's Nothing Stronger Than Our Love" in 1975?

15. And what song popularized the phrase *"Voulez-vous coucher avec moi ce soir"*?

(answers on page 215)

Goodbye, Vietnam

1. Four students were killed at Kent State in 1970. How many were wounded?

2. At what other campus were 14 people shot, two fatally, also while protesting the U.S. invasion of Cambodia?

3. After he announced the invasion, what did Richard Nixon put around the White House to keep antiwar protesters out?

4. And what governor, commenting on student demonstrations that year, said, "If it's a bloodbath they want, let's get it over with"?

5. In 1971 Daniel Ellsberg gave the Nixon administration a headache. What did he give *The New York Times*?

6. And what did the Nixon administration do in response?

7. After President Nixon ordered the mining and bombing of Haiphong harbor in North Vietnam, what did the 1972 Nixon campaign spend $8,000 to send to the White House?

8. Name the president who ended draft registration and the president who started it again.

9. Why, beginning in 1971, were all American servicemen returning from Vietnam subject to urinalysis tests?

10. Why did Nixon play down a letter-writing campaign to gain him the 1973 Nobel Peace Prize? (Hint: It wasn't modesty.)

11. Who actually won the prize?

12. Who, in January 1970, offered North Vietnam $100 million of his own money as ransom for American POWs?

13. The longest and most contentious court-martial in U.S. history ended March 29, 1971, with the conviction of whom for what?
14. What song, played on Armed Forces radio, was the signal for the final U.S. evacuation of Saigon on April 30, 1975?
15. What was Saigon renamed after the Communist victory?

(answers on page 215)

True Or False? 3

Eight of the following 10 items are true. Can you ferret out the two fakes?

1. Although not successful in his presidential bid, Morris the Cat visited the White House and signed a bill with his paw.
2. Olga Korbut went to the Munich Olympics as a stand-in for another Soviet gymnast who had been injured.
3. E. Howard Hunt and G. Gordon Liddy considered a plot to discredit columnist Jack Anderson by putting a chemical on the steering wheel of his car that, when absorbed by his skin, would cause him to become rambling and incoherent.
4. Virgil Cleves was arrested in 1974 for strolling in Lima, Ohio's public square in the nude, and charged with public indecency. The 67-year-old Cleves told police that he was too old for streaking and said that for older people the term should be "snailing."
5. In the 1979 World Series, Fidel Castro was rooting for the Baltimore Orioles.
6. Male hygiene deodorants, a.k.a. crotch sprays, were introduced in 1970 with such names as Pub Below the Belt and Bill Blass' Man's Other Deodorant.
7. When scientists wanted to include the sound of a kiss on the Voyager records, NASA told them to make sure that it sounded heterosexual.
8. The polyester leisure suit began to go out of favor after certain cheap imports proved highly flammable and three men suffered severe burns in separate incidents, two while smoking and one while cooking steaks on a hibachi.
9. In 1971 the Texas House of Representatives passed a resolution commending the Boston Strangler, Albert DeSalvo,

for his efforts in the field of population control.

10. As of 1970, a married woman in California needed court approval to engage in an independent business.

(answers on page 216)

TV 9

1. This program was probably the only place on the air where a man dressed as a turkey could lay plastic eggs while playing "Turkey in the Straw" on the harmonica. Name it.
2. Whose favorite drink was grape Nehi?
3. Where was Dennis McCloud from?
4. Where did the Partridge Family live?
5. *The Odd Couple* were Oscar Madison and Felix Unger, but who were their ex-wives?
6. Peter Falk was the producers' second choice to play *Columbo*. Who was their first choice?
7. Who was Bumper Morgan?
8. What health expert died of a heart attack during a taping of *The Dick Cavett Show*?
9. After Sonny and Cher got their divorce in 1974, they quit their show, *The Sonny and Cher Comedy Hour*. What shows did they go on to star in?
10. What was the name of the chubby waitress who worked at Rob's soda shop on *What's Happening!!* and who played her?
11. On *The Betty White Show*, Betty White played Joyce Whitman, an actress who had her own series. What was Joyce Whitman's TV show called?
12. What caused Barnaby Jones to come out of retirement?
13. Who was the first person to be granted freedom on *Roots*?
14. After these two "jiggle shows" were attacked by the National Federation for Decency, Sears pulled its ads from them. Name the two programs.
15. Who was Buttons?

(answers on page 216)

Who was *Carrie* White's (Sissy Spacek's) date to the prom?

Answer:
Tommy Ross (William Katt)

News 4

1. Who defended his wining and dining of a visiting Libyan "friendship delegation" in 1979 with the words, "There is a hell of a lot more Arabians than there is Jews"?

2. What did Michael Carvin aim at Ronald Reagan on November 20, 1975?

3. When the Khirov and Bolshoi ballets left Canada in 1974, what did they leave behind?

4. Name the magazine that began publication in 1974, reportedly with $20,000 in drug money.

5. Facing declining sales due to an ongoing boycott, California grape growers finally capitulated in July 1970 to demands that the United Farm Workers Union be recognized. What crop did Cesar Chavez and the UFW start boycotting the next month?

6. This foreign leader declared himself King of Scotland, but the queen was none too amused. Who was he?

7. In March 1977, members of a religious sect held 132 people hostage in Washington, D.C., for 38 hours because they were upset about the opening of a movie. Who were they, and what was the movie?

8. After burning for 24 hours, what sank in Hong Kong harbor in 1972?

9. Who dressed up as "Pogo the Clown," and how many boys did he kill before his arrest in 1978?

10. Who was "Mr. Up and Coming Republican," and why was he sentenced to death in 1979?

11. Most people want to get out of jail, but these people refused to leave Alcatraz; and in June 1971 federal marshals were forced to evict them. Who were they?

12. What was Youth Explo '72?

13. "May Allah cure you," one sympathetic well-wisher wrote President Carter from Egypt in late 1978. "This illness should have been inflicted on an unjust leader rather than you, O Carter." With what malady was the president afflicted, causing him to cancel appointments for a day?

14. The '60s had the Chicago Seven. The '70s had this group of eight, who were acquitted of charges that they had conspired to disrupt the 1972 Republican convention by such means as shooting incendiary devices from slingshots and

crossbows. By what name was the group known?

15. In 1974 the government of China condemned his teachings and declared them to be reactionary. Who was he?

(answers on page 217)

Quotes 4

Who said:

1. "Between you and me and the gatepost, Mr. President always knew [about Watergate]."

   a. Martha Mitchell
   b. David Eisenhower
   c. Bebe Rebozo
   d. Rose Mary Woods

2. "Watergate was worse than a crime, it was a blunder."

   a. Henry Kissinger
   b. Leonid Brezhnev
   c. G. Gordon Liddy
   d. Richard Nixon

3. "The illegal we do immediately. The unconstitutional takes a little longer."

   a. Richard Daley
   b. Richard Nixon
   c. Henry Kissinger
   d. Ferdinand Marcos

4. "When the president does it, that means it is not illegal."

   a. Sammy Davis, Jr.
   b. Bob Hope
   c. John Wayne
   d. Richard Nixon

5. "I changed my registration from Republican to Democrat before I went to prison because I couldn't stand the idea of a Republican going to jail."

   a. H. R. Haldeman
   b. Charles Colson
   c. John Ehrlichman
   d. Ted Bundy

6. "It could have been a hell of a lot worse. They could have sentenced me to spend the rest of my life with Martha Mitchell."

    a. *Maurice Stans*
    b. *E. Howard Hunt*
    c. *Richard Nixon*
    d. *John Mitchell*

7. "I don't believe in that 'no comment' business. I always have a comment."

    a. *Betty Ford*
    b. *Bella Abzug*
    c. *Spiro Agnew*
    d. *Martha Mitchell*

8. "A great many people think that polysyllables are a sign of intelligence."

    a. *Barbara Walters*
    b. *Spiro Agnew*
    c. *William F. Buckley, Jr.*
    d. *Sylvester Stallone*

9. "I'm astounded by people who take 18 years to write something. That's how long it took that guy to write *Madam Bovary*, and was that ever on the best-seller list? No, it was a lousy book and it made a lousy movie."

    a. *Judith Krantz*
    b. *Harold Robbins*
    c. *Jackie Collins*
    d. *Sylvester Stallone*

10. "Every French town has an Avenue Victor Hugo. We never have Mark Twain Street."

    a. *Joyce Carol Oates*
    b. *Saul Bellow*
    c. *Barbara Tuchman*
    d. *Hunter S. Thompson*

11. "Football is about the only unifying force left in America today."

    a. *Woody Hayes*
    b. *John Madden*
    c. *Pete Rozelle*
    d. *Gerald Ford*

12. "I've often thought with Nixon that if he'd made the football team, his life would have been different."

    a. *Gerald Ford*
    b. *Adela Rogers St. John*
    c. *Shana Alexander*
    d. *Joe Namath*

13. "Of course, Behaviorism 'works.' So does torture. Give me a no-nonsense, down-to-earth behaviorist, a few drugs, and simple electrical appliances, and in six months I will have him reciting the Athanasian Creed in public."

    a. *W. H. Auden*
    b. *B. F. Skinner*
    c. *Carl Rogers*
    d. *Augusto Pinochet*

14. "We wish to avoid at all costs the recurrent experience in some democratic countries where the people give the governments the opposition they deserve."

    a. *Mohammad Reza Pahlavi*
    b. *Ferdinand Marcos*
    c. *Nguyen van Thieu*
    d. *Richard Nixon*

15. "The greatest freedom I enjoy is the freedom from life-insurance salesmen."

    a. *Evel Knievel*
    b. *Paul "Red" Adair*
    c. *A. J. Foyt*
    d. *Gary Gilmore*

(answers on page 219)

People 5

1. Why did it seem for a while that Melvin Dummar might become a very, very rich man?
2. In 1975 Yelena Bonner was given the Nobel Peace Prize. But it wasn't awarded to her. How did this happen?
3. What did J. Paul Getty III lose in Italy?
4. Did film director Roman Polanski serve any time for his molestation of a 13-year-old girl in 1977?
5. In 1973 the International Gymnastics Federation threatened to ban some of

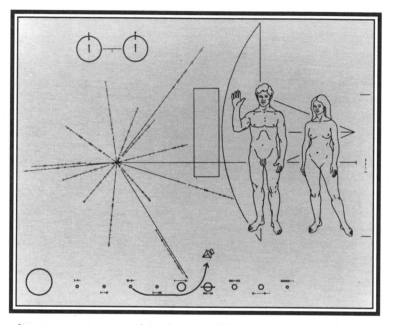

Someday space aliens may encounter this plate from Pioneer II. Identify the four main messages we Earthlings are trying to get across.

Answer: 1) The figures on the right represent the creatures who built Pioneer, which is shown in the back-ground. 2) At the bottom the sun and planets of our solar system are represented, showing from which planet Pioneer was sent and at what trajectory. 3) The radiating lines on the left show the positions of 14 pulsars, which are sources of radio energy, relative to the sun (in center) at the time of Pioneer's launch. The "1-" marks are binary numbers that represent the frequencies of the pulsars at the time of launch. 4) At the upper left is depicted a hydrogen atom with a clock so that aliens, using the binary numbers, can figure out the regular decrease in the frequencies of the pulsars, and thus the time elapsed since Pioneer's launch.

this gymnast's moves as too dangerous. Whose?

6. This Miss America of 1971, whose good
luck charm was a pet hermit crab,
went on to become the first prime-time
female sports broadcaster. Name her.

7. Who was Governor Moonbeam?

8. Who was Senator Moon Rock?

9. Name the artist whose exhibit *The Dinner Party* was a tribute to real and
mythological "lost" heroines of history.

10. What happened to Bob Hall in November 1972 when both his parachute and
reserve chute failed to open, and he
dropped 3,300 feet at speeds of up to 80
miles an hour?

11. Who married Philippe Junot?

12. Why did David Eisenhower not attend
his commencement ceremony at
Amherst College in June 1970?

13. Who was *Time* magazine's Man of the
Year for 1975?

14. What famous figure surprised onlook-
ers by saying "woo woo" during his
visit to the U.S.?

15. Who was Lucy, and why was she famous?

(answers on page 218)

20 More Songs From Hell

Below are 20 more hit songs that the
planet is still suffering through on eleva-
tors. Unlike our previous list, the performers of these ditties are generally well
known. You should be able to recall them
from memory, which will give your brain
something to do besides repeat, endlessly,
such refrains as "The Candy Man can
'cause he mixes it with love and makes the
world taste good."

1. "The Candy Man"
2. "Paper Roses"
3. "(You're) Having My Baby"
4. "The Happiest Girl in the Whole
   U.S.A."
5. "A Horse With No Name"
6. "Midnight at the Oasis"
7. "Watching Scotty Grow"
8. "Go Away Little Girl"
9. "Torn Between Two Lovers"
10. "Before the Next Teardrop Falls"
11. "Daddy Don't You Walk So Fast"
12. "The Morning After"
13. "Laughter in the Rain"
14. "Muskrat Love"
15. "Everything Is Beautiful"
16. "I Shot the Sheriff"

17. "Alone Again, Naturally"
18. "Undercover Angel"
19. "Me and My Arrow"
20. "Funny Face"

(answers on page 220)

Sports 3

1. In 1979 it became the longest touchdown pass in Super Bowl history. Who threw it, who caught it, and how long was it?
2. After winning the Triple Crown in 1977, Seattle Slew was made an honorary citizen by the governor of what state?
3. Name the golfer who, in 1971, became the first person to win the British, U.S., and Canadian Opens in the same year.
4. And what did he throw at rival Jack Nicklaus on the last day of the U.S. Open?
5. Oakland A's owner Charlie O. Finley gave his team a mascot in 1972. What was it, and what did he name it?
6. Ann Meyers was the first woman to do what?
7. This was, by the end of the decade, the fastest-growing participatory sport in America, up 283 percent from 1976 to 1979. What sport was it?
8. What did Ted Giannoulas pretend to do to umpires?
9. In 1975 she swam around Manhattan in 7 hours and 57 minutes. In 1978 she tried swimming from Cuba to Florida, but gave up after 42 hours when adverse winds drove her too far off course. In 1979 she became the first person to swim from the Bahamas to Florida. Who was she?
10. Name the U.S. athlete who was granted a visa to play in South Africa in 1973 but was refused hotel accommodations.
11. What was unusual about baseballs in 1974?
12. Who did the Women's Tennis Association insist pass a chromosome test before being allowed into major tournaments in 1977?
13. This New York Nets basketball star rejected nicknames such as "Houdini," "The Claw," and "Black Moses." Who

was he, and what did he prefer to be called?

14. What was unusual about Bonnie Sloan, who played for the St. Louis Cardinals in 1973?

15. What did Gary Muhrcke do in 12 minutes and 32 seconds in Manhattan in 1978?

(answers on page 220)

Movies 9

1. What did Bobby Duprea (Jack Nicholson) order at the diner in *Five Easy Pieces*?

2. In *M*A*S*H*, what did the other doctors give "Painless" the dentist (John Schuck) to commit suicide with?

3. In *Two Mules for Sister Sara*, when was the attack on the French garrison in Chihuahua planned, and why?

4. What box office smash did Anthony Daniels and Kenny Baker star in, and whom did they play?

5. What film was shot at the Voyager Motel in North Miami Beach, Florida?

6. Joan Rivers made her directorial debut with this 1978 movie about the first pregnant man. Name it.

7. In *The Turning Point*, Emma (Anne Bancroft) and Deedee (Shirley MacLaine) had been vying for the lead in the ballet *Anna Karenina*. Deedee got pregnant. What did Emma get?

8. This 1978 film starred Donny and Marie Osmond. Name it, and name the characters they played.

9. What was the name of the "thing" that was threatening the galaxy in *Star Trek—The Motion Picture*?

10. Why did Margo Sperling (Lily Tomlin) hire Ira Wells (Art Carney) in *The Late Show*?

11. Who played Loretta Lynn in *Coal Miner's Daughter*, and who did the singing?

12. Director Federico Fellini's *Amarcord* was a nostalgic look at the Italy of his youth. The word *amarcord* means something in his hometown dialect. What?

13. Brooke Shields played 12-year-old prostitute Violet in what 1978 film?

14. Why did Thomas Jerome Newton (David Bowie) come to Earth in _The Man Who Fell to Earth_?
15. What movie ended with the line, "A baadasssss nigger is coming back to collect some dues"?

(answers on page 221)

Numbers—Women

Match the correct number to each item.

1. Of the 90,000 school systems in the U.S. in 1973, the number in which women were superintendent
2. The number of dollars by which a man's median income exceeded a woman's in 1974
3. In 1976, the percentage of secretaries who were women
4. As of 1977, the percentage of on-camera network correspondents who were women
5. The number of battered women's shelters in the U.S. in 1973
6. The number of battered women's shelters in the U.S. six years later
7. The average number of deaths of women per 100,000 abortions, according to a 1977 Centers for Disease Control report
8. The average number of deaths of women per 100,000 births, according to the same report
9. Of the 62 TV shows in 1973 with regularly appearing leading performers, the number with women leads
10. The number of women who served in Richard Nixon's cabinet

    _a. 0_
    _b. 0_
    _c. 6,052_
    _d. 8_
    _e. 2.5_
    _f. 250_
    _g. 98_
    _h. 6_
    _i. 13_
    _j. 13_

(answers on page 221)

Jerry Reed and Burt Reynolds fend off the critics—or was it the fashion police?—in this 1976 film, Reynolds' directorial debut. Name it.

Answer:
Gator

Jimmy Carter

He had big white teeth. He carried his own luggage. He wore jeans and cardigans, and his brother wore a hat made of beer can pop-tops. But the common touch wore thin as events conspired against him, and, economically speaking, he left the country with peanuts.

1. President Carter signed an amnesty bill restoring the citizenship of a famous former American. Who? (Clue: The guy was dead.)
2. Match the member of the Carter family with the appropriate occupation:

   a. *Convicted felon*
   b. *Georgia state legislator*
   c. *Peace Corps volunteer*
   d. *Faith healer*
   e. *Peanut warehouse manager*

   1. Billy Carter
   2. William Carter Spann
   3. Ruth Carter Stapleton
   4. Lillian Carter
   5. Hugh Carter

3. Which Carter lost in 1976?
4. What did Jimmy tell *Playboy* that he sometimes had in his heart?
5. And during his visit to Poland in 1977, what feelings did he have for the Polish people, as described by an improper translation at the time?
6. Why was Gloria Carter Spann, the president's younger sister, arrested at McWaffle's restaurant in Americus, Georgia, in 1978?
7. Gustatorily speaking, what couldn't you get at the Carter White House?
8. With which of the following two people did Rosalynn Carter *not* pose for a photo?

   a. *David Berkowitz*
   b. *Reverend Jim Jones*
   c. *Idi Amin*
   d. *John Wayne Gacy*

9. Carter could get no rest in 1979. Even a fishing trip went awry when he was forced to fend off a crazed, "killer" _____, which was swimming angrily toward his boat. What?
10. On what TV game show did Carter appear two years before his election?

11. Fill in the blank: *Why Not* _____ _____?
12. Why didn't Carter light the national Christmas tree in December 1979?
13. Carter said he enjoyed listening to music by which four of the following:

    a. *Bob Dylan*
    b. *The Ramones*
    c. *Led Zeppelin*
    d. *The Allman Brothers*
    e. *The Grateful Dead*

14. There was nothing quite like the sound of Carter's Spanish, spoken with a flat Southern drawl. While the Mexicans may or may not have been thrilled with his accent, they were definitely less than pleased by some comments he made on a visit to Mexico in 1979. What did he say?
15. Years later, when Hillary Rodham Clinton did it, nobody seemed to care. But when Rosalynn Carter tried it, such a ruckus was raised that she had to stop. What did she do?

(answers on page 222)

Who Did What? 2

1. Mark Rifkin
2. Robert Anson
3. Sally Stanford
4. Junko Tabei
5. Harold J. Haley
6. Ted Patrick
7. Jeffrey MacDonald
8. Billy Hayes
9. Jacqueline Means
10. Chris Sizemore
11. Hope Cooke
12. Dita Beard
13. John Singlaub
14. Paul MacCready
15. Benjamin Mendoza

    a. *Deprogrammer of cult members*
    b. *Sikkim queen—and former U.S. citizen—forced to flee her country in 1973*
    c. *ITT scandal lobbyist*
    d. *Would-be assassin of Pope Paul VI in 1970*
    e. *Time correspondent held captive in Cambodia*

f. American, subject of Midnight Express, imprisoned
in Turkey for smuggling
hashish

g. First woman to climb to the
top of Mount Everest

h. Computer analyst who illegally transferred $10 mil-
lion from a U.S. bank to his
Swiss bank account

i. General removed from
command for publicly op-
posing Carter's South Ko-
rea policy

j. California Superior Court
judge taken hostage by
convicts during trial and
killed in shootout

k. Former San Francisco
madam who became
mayor of Sausalito, Cali-
fornia

l. First woman Episcopal
priest in U.S.

m. Doctor and ex–Green Beret
convicted of killing his wife
and two daughters

n. Woman who revealed she
was Eve in The Three
Faces of Eve

o. Designer of the Gossamer
Albatross, first human-
powered aircraft to cross
the English Channel

(answers on page 222)

TV 10

1. Name the original Not Ready for Prime
Time Players.

2. In this, one of the most popular made-
for-TV movies of all time, editor Lyman
Spencer (Bert Convy) assigned reporter Laura Coleman (Jane Seymour)
to get the behind-the-scenes, inside
story on . . . what?

3. Who was Sam the butcher?

4. What was the occupation of Stewart
McMillan on McMillan and Wife? What
had been the occupation of Sally
McMillan's father?

5. Who were officers Terry Webster, Mike
Danko, and Willie Gillis?

6. What program featured periodic ap-
pearances by Mrs. Buffalo Running
Schwartz?

7. Who defended Dr. Steven Kiley, of *Marcus Welby, M.D.*, against a paternity suit?
8. Why was Shaaron Claridge's voice famous?
9. Name the unsuccessful American knockoff of *Upstairs, Downstairs*.
10. For whom was the character Fred Sanford named in *Sanford and Son*?
11. What was the name of the never-seen, intoxicated doorman on *Rhoda*? Who played him?
12. Who were Happy Kyne and the Mirth Makers?
13. This short-lived TV show, which tried to cash in on the success of *Saturday Night Fever*, did manage to produce a hit song sung by the show's star, David Naughton. Give the name of the show or the song (they're the same).
14. Who were Jeremy Gelbwaks, Brian Forster, and Suzanne Crough?
15. What was Hawkeye's real name on *M*A*S*H*?

(answers on page 223)

The Oscars

1. This 1975 movie swept all five major Academy Awards (Best Picture, Best Director, Best Screenplay, Best Actor, and Best Actress), the only film of the decade and the first film since 1934 to do so. What was it?
2. Name the "Apache" woman sent by Marlon Brando to refuse the 1972 Best Actor award on his behalf "because of the treatment of Indians by the film industry."
3. Actually, she wasn't really a Native American at all but a little-known actress who had once been named "Miss American Vampire of 1970." What was her *real* name?
4. In 1974 this 10-year-old became the youngest person ever to win an Academy Award. Who was she, and what film did she win for?
5. Robert Opel stole the show at the 1974 Oscar ceremony. How?
6. In 1976 she became the first woman in Academy history to be nominated for Best Director. Who was she, and what film was she nominated for?
7. What Best Supporting Actress winner caused a ruckus at the 1978 awards

ceremony by complaining during her acceptance speech about the "small bunch of Zionist hoodlums" who were outside protesting her involvement in a pro-Palestinian documentary?

8. Later, during that same ceremony, the awards presenter for Best Original Screenplay was so angry at her remarks that he rebuked her from the stage. "I'm sick and tired of people exploiting the Academy Awards for the propagation of their own personal propaganda," he said, when "a simple 'Thank you' would have sufficed." At that, he angrily tore open the envelope without ever mentioning the nominees. Who was he?

9. This was the only sequel ever to win an Academy Award for Best Picture. Name it.

10. To whom was the Academy's first posthumous award made?

11. What unusual group accompanied Debby Boone in her rendition of "You Light Up My Life" at the 1978 awards ceremony?

12. And what was later found to be *particularly* odd about them?

13. Director Luis Buñuel scandalized Hollywood by jokingly saying that since he had bribed the Academy with $25,000, he wouldn't be surprised when he won an Oscar. Despite this, he won anyway, for Best Foreign Film of 1972. Name the film.

14. In 1973 host Charlton Heston had a flat tire on the freeway and wasn't there for the start of the ceremony. What famous macho actor was put on the spot when he was suddenly pulled from the audience to host in Heston's place?

15. In 1974 Katharine Hepburn presented the Irving Thalberg Award to producer Lawrence Weingarten. What was unusual about her doing so?

(answers on page 223)

Songs 3

From these first lines, name the songs and the people who performed them.

1. "Hey, girl, watcha doin' down there?"
2. "Good morning morning, hello sunshine, wake up sleepyhead."
3. "I got chills, they're multiplyin'."
4. "I have a mansion but forget the price."

5. "Looking out at the road rushing under my wheels."
6. "Mem'ries light the corners of my mind."
7. "Daylight, all right!"
8. "When are you gonna come down, when are you going to land?"
9. "Well, you can tell by the way I use my walk, I'm a woman's man, no time to talk."
10. "So you think you're a Romeo, playing a part in a picture show."
11. "My child arrived just the other day."
12. "We all came out to Montreaux on the Lake Genova shoreline."
13. "We don't need no education."
14. "Shake it up, shake it down."
15. "See the curtains hangin' in the window in the evening on a Friday night."

(answers on page 224)

The Environment

1. Why did hundreds of students smash a new car to pieces at Northern Illinois University, De Kalb, on April 22, 1970?
2. What was the Tecopa pupfish's claim to fame?
3. In 1974 a suspicious auto accident claimed the life of a plutonium-industry worker who was spilling the (radioactive) beans to reporters about conditions at her place of employment. Who was she, and what company did she work for?
4. What did the Food and Drug Administration tell people not to eat due to mercury contamination in 1971?
5. Honolulu was the only one of the nation's 105 largest population centers to meet these standards, according to a 1978 Environmental Protection Agency study. What standards?
6. In 1976 the James River Corporation was fined $13 million for contaminating the James River with what chemical?
7. In response to the Arab oil embargo in 1973, the U.S. Senate voted 49–48 to approve this controversial project. What was it?

What are these men searching for?

Answer:
The duck that lays golden eggs, in the movie $1,000,000 Duck

8. Why was fishing banned in the Hudson River in 1976?
9. In 1971 a commission blamed this as the major cause of pollution in Lake Erie. What?
10. To what did Italian authorities attribute a rash of breast enlargements that affected 213 boys and 110 girls at one school in 1979?
11. Why did the U.S. Supreme Court stop construction of the Tellico Dam on the Little Tennessee River in 1978?
12. In 1071, responding to the concerns of environmentalists, Congress decided that while it might have been OK for the French, the British, and the Soviets, it would be too noisy for Americans. What was it?
13. From what New York community were people evacuated in 1978 when it was discovered that their homes were built over an abandoned toxic waste dump site?
14. It was a propellant in hair sprays and an ingredient in the manufacture of dentures, shower curtains, and phonograph records. It was also found, in 1975, to be causing a rare liver cancer, not to mention brain, blood, and genetic abnormalities. What was it?

15. Three Mile Island may have been the decade's most famous nuclear accident, but it wasn't necessarily the most dangerous: In 1975 a fire crippled the nation's largest reactor and left it only hours away from meltdown. Name the reactor.

(answers on page 224)

Advertising

1. What, in 1971, did the Federal Trade Commission ask the makers of Wonder Bread to prove?
2. Why did Arthur Godfrey decide to stop hawking Axion detergent in 1970?
3. Who was famous for wearing Beauty Mist pantyhose in TV commercials?
4. What was billed as weighing 7 pounds, 11 ounces, just right for putting on your stomach?
5. What was "prime quality for $1.26 a pound" and would have killed you had you put it on your stomach?
6. In 1970 Mexican-American groups finally convinced Frito-Lay to stop run-

ning commercials featuring what cartoon character?

7. What brand of cigarettes featured a photo of Charlie Chaplin on the package and ad copy that read "Buy 'Em or Bum 'Em. . . . They're nice. They're lovable"? (Yes, not unlike kittens, puppies, and bunnies, a *lovable* cigarette.)

8. Who asked if we had ever eaten a pine tree?

9. What airline experienced a 23 percent increase in passengers from 1971 to 1972, partially as a result of an ad campaign that announced "Hi, I'm Cheryl. Fly Me to Miami."

10. Irate flight attendants walked out of the 1974 press conference at which Continental Air Lines, evidently inspired by the success of its competitor's "Fly Me" campaign, introduced a new slogan. What was it?

11. What three-year-old could be counted on to like Life cereal?

12. Although he became better known for his hit pop tunes, this singer/songwriter left his mark on the TV airwaves with jingles such as Kentucky Fried Chicken's "Get a Bucket of Chicken/Have a Barrel of Fun" and the immortal "(And Like a Good Neighbor) State Farm Is There." Who was he?

13. Who reminded us that Paul Masson would sell no wine before its time?

14. What pudgy-faced, red-haired child sold Underwood Chicken Spread, Post Raisin Bran, Oscar Meyer bologna, and other products in the early '70s, for which he earned three Clio awards?

15. In 1971 she became a household name in the bedroom as well as the laundry room when her porno film *Beyond the Green Door* arrived in movie theaters just as millions of boxes of Ivory Soap with her picture on the front arrived in supermarkets. Who was she?

(answers on page 225)

Real Shows? 2

Here are 10 more unusual plots for TV shows. Nine are real. Which is the fake, and what were the names of the real shows?

1. In this comedy, a young science teacher inherits an inn only to discover that its caretaker is the original Frankenstein monster and that he himself is the great-great-grandson of the original Dr. Frankenstein. The monster convinces him to keep the inn open and to try to duplicate his ancestor's research. Guests may be advised to avoid annoying the bellhop.

2. An aging billionaire tries to hunt down a handsome young race-car driver who just happens to be immortal. The hero's blood contains antibodies to disease and old age, making it particularly attractive to elderly, evil rich people.

3. A man, declared legally dead seven years after deserting his family, moves into the same apartment building as his "widow" and tries to win her back. He also tries to get himself declared legally alive.

4. A music promoter offers two young rock musicians a chance at stardom—with one catch. The promoter is the son of the Devil (perhaps not too surprising in show business), and in exchange for a year of superstardom, the musicians will have to sign away their souls. To tempt them into signing the contract, the promoter gives them small tastes of what fame will be like.

5. Bored with their lives, a middle-class couple decide that they need a change, so they get work as a butler and a cook for an extremely wealthy family. Although they're obviously inexperienced, their boss decides to keep them anyway. His snobbish sister, however, is irritated by their incompetence and is constantly looking for ways to get them fired.

6. When sheep—along with the occasional farmer—start mysteriously being killed, no one thinks of suspecting the new high-school football coach, who has an unfortunate habit of turning into a werewolf. Things are complicated by the coach's romance with the female sheriff, who is trying to solve the killings.

7. A woman caring for her five orphaned nieces and nephews decides to take in a boarder to help meet expenses. Unbeknown to her, however, her boarder is an angel, albeit an incompetent one, who has been sent to help her out. The kids soon discover the boarder's secret.

8. Ten years in the future, world governments have established that unidentified flying objects pose a threat to Earth. The public doesn't know this yet, so a secret multinational defense center is set up under a movie studio (well, why not?) to battle the aliens and keep Earth safe.

9. An accident-prone cop keeps sending partners to the hospital, so the department teams him up with a lifelike robot that the cop isn't supposed to know isn't human. The cop figures it out, of course, because his partner has the unique ability to spit out color photographs and is once short-circuited by a criminal's bullet, which causes him to tap-dance wildly during a chase.

10. The last survivor of Atlantis joins a group of modern-day scientists to study undersea life. Since he's an Atlantean, not only does he come equipped with webbed hands and feet and superhuman strength, but he also has gills— which puts a crimp in his social life since he must return to the sea periodically to breathe.

(answers on page 226)

People 6

1. Arkansas evangelist David Aaron Rogers said in 1978, "We tried everything Jesus told us to do and we don't know what went wrong." What had he been trying to do?

2. Indian Prime Minister Morarji Desai had an unusual cure for cancer and cataracts, and he even claimed that it had cured his brother of tuberculosis. This therapy, he said, "is very good for you, and it is even free." What was his cure?

3. New York Yankee pitchers Mike Kekich and Fritz Peterson were such good friends that they shared many things with each other. What was the one thing they shared during the early '70s that one of their wives called "the most unique trade in baseball history"?

4. What caused Karen Ann Quinlan's coma?

5. Elizabeth Ray worked for a congressman, although she admitted, "I can't type. I can't file. I can't even answer the phone." Whom did she work for and what did she do?
6. What chess champion thought that the CIA was poisoning his yogurt and trying to psych him out with gamma rays?
7. Who was Richard Dixon?
8. In 1973, 100-year-old Johnnie Lee Fegion filed for divorce from her husband of 28 years, Solomon, 103, on what grounds?
9. What did astronaut Edgar Mitchell do during his Apollo 14 lunar expedition that embarrassed some people at NASA?
10. And what astronaut retired from the space program "to spend more time spreading the good news of Jesus Christ"?
11. This politician became famous for such alliterative phrases as "vicars of vacillation," "hopeless, hysterical hypochondriacs of history," "pusillanimous pussyfooters," and "nattering nabobs of negativism." Name him.
12. What did Robert Le Clair, 24, brunet, 36-30-32, win in 1972?
13. Who was Vladimir "Spider" Sabich?

14. Why did Carter drug advisor Peter Bourne resign in 1978?
15. Who officiated at history's largest mass wedding, and how many couples got married?

(answers on page 226)

Numbers—News

Match the correct number to each item.

1. In May 1970, the percentage of Americans polled who opposed the Vietnam War, which ended three years later
2. The number of American citizens on which the CIA admitted having illegal files as of 1975
3. The number of POWs who returned from Vietnam during "Operation Homecoming" in 1973
4. The number of Vietnamese refugees flown to the U.S. in 1975 after the fall of South Vietnam
5. The number of years in prison to which Patty Hearst was sentenced for bank robbery
6. The number of wills filed within a few weeks of the death of Howard Hughes

in 1976 that claimed a share of the billionaire's estate

7. The number of sleeping pills found in
the stomach of rock drummer Keith
Moon of the Who after his death from
an overdose of the same in 1978
8. The number of bad welds and ruptures
found on the Alaska pipeline during its
trial run in 1976
9. The national speed limit originally suggested by President Nixon in response
to the 1973 Arab oil embargo
10. The percentage increase in Texaco's
profits from the fourth quarter of 1972,
before the embargo, to the fourth quarter of 1973, when the embargo was in
force

    a. 24
    b. 514
    c. 10,000
    d. 140,000
    e. 32
    f. 60
    g. 50
    h. 70
    i. 7
    j. 3,955

(answers on page 227)

TV 11

1. What was unusual about the spaceship on *Space: 1999*?
2. Who was Huggy Bear?
3. Name the program that offered a
"Lovemate of the Week"—a video "centerfold" featuring a different woman
each episode.
4. Mary Tyler Moore starred in three TV
series during the '70s. Of course you remember *The Mary Tyler Moore Show*,
but what were the names of the other
two programs?
5. What was the name of Geraldine's
boyfriend on *The Flip Wilson Show*?
6. Who was trying to restore the boat *The
Answer*?
7. Why did Chico leave Ed's Garage to
go into business with his father during
the last season of *Chico and the Man*?
8. Who was Exidor?
9. What TV station was owned by Guy
Caballero and managed by Edith
Prickley?
10. On *All in the Family*, what was the
Stivics' baby named?
11. Who lived at 165 Eaton Place, London?
12. What caused mild-mannered David
Banner to become *The Incredible
Hulk*?

13. *It Happened One Christmas*, starring Marlo Thomas, was a TV-movie remake of what famous 1946 film?
14. What was the name of Margaret Pynchon's Yorkie?
15. On *60 Minutes*, who were the two columnists on "Point Counterpoint"?

(answers on page 227)

Music 6

1. What was the last single that Elvis recorded before he died? (Hint: Sid Vicious did a version of the same song a few years later.)
2. *Tommy* may have been more famous, but who wrote the 1979 rock opera *Joe's Garage?*
3. *Billboard* magazine described this brother-sister duo as "the most successful American act during the '70s." Who were they?
4. Name the performer who began the first of his annual country music "picnics" on July 4, 1973, in Dripping Springs, Texas.
5. In the 1974 hit "TSOP" by MFSB, what did all those initials stand for?
6. Sixteen members of this orchestra asked to be excused from playing at President Nixon's 1973 inauguration because they opposed his Vietnam War policies. And almost half of the orchestra objected to the warlike nature of one of the works scheduled for the program. Name the orchestra and the controversial piece.
7. Speaking of the classics, which two of the following were not used as the bases for disco songs?

   a. Mussorgsky's "Night on Bald Mountain"
   b. Grieg's "Peer Gynt" suite
   c. Wagner's "Ride of the Valkyries"
   d. Beethoven's Fifth Symphony
   e. Rimsky-Korsakov's "Flight of the Bumble Bee"

8. With what tune did Herb Alpert make a comeback in 1979?
9. Who was Ziggy Stardust?
10. Who sang 1978's "Nanu, Nanu (I Wanna Funcky Wich You)"?

Who were these characters on *Mary Hart-man, Mary Hartman*, and what was their relationship to Mary?

Answer: Top row, from left to right: Tom Hartman (husband), Martha Shumway (mother), Mary Hartman, Raymond Larkin (grandfather). Bottom row, from left to right: Heather Hartman (daughter), George Shumway (father), Cathy Shumway (sister).

11. What happened at the 1974 Country Music Association awards that led some performers to form their own group, the Association of Country Entertainers?

12. Name the Boomtown Rats song based on a shooting incident in San Diego in January 1979 in which a teenager killed two people at a school.

13. The Band, Joni Mitchell, Joan Baez, and Arlo Guthrie starred in this revue that toured with Bob Dylan in the mid-'70s. What was it called?

14. Why did Lynyrd Skynyrd change the cover of its *Street Survivor* LP, which showed the band enveloped in flames, shortly after the album came out in 1977?

15. In June 1977, this rock star's planned tour was almost derailed when his boa constrictor was mortally bitten by the live rat it had been fed for breakfast. Who was the rocker, and how did he solve his snake problem?

(answers on page 228)

First Lines 4

Match the first line with the book it came from.

1. "It was morning, and the new sun sparkled gold across the ripples of a gentle sea."

2. "In this aurora-pinkish lighting, everyone said, even the *boeuf en gelée* looked younger."

3. "For some time now they had been suspicious of him."

4. "In those days cheap apartments were almost impossible to find in Manhattan, so I had to move to Brooklyn."

5. "Whole sight; or all the rest is desolation."

6. "On December 8th, 1915, Maggie Cleary had her fourth birthday."

7. "The dust-grimed window of the office building facing New York's Times Square reflected, as through a looking glass, an extraordinary corner of Wonderland."

8. "Gary Cooper White was born in Jersey City, New Jersey."

9. "We are told that the trouble with Modern Man is that he has been trying to detach himself from nature."
10. "It is true that the sex of a person is attested by every cell in his body."
11. "This is the tale of a meeting of two lonesome, skinny, fairly old white men on a planet which was dying fast."
12. "I recall with utter clarity the first great shock of my life."
13. "The hull of the submarine was lashed to the huge pilings, a behemoth strapped in silhouette, the sweeping lines of its bow arcing into the light of the North Sea dawn."
14. "I was making a film about a dying woman."
15. "The world is very old, and human beings are very young."

    a. The Thorn Birds *by Colleen McCullough*
    b. Breakfast of Champions *by Kurt Vonnegut, Jr.*
    c. The Female Eunuch *by Germaine Greer*
    d. The Holcroft Covenant *by Robert Ludlum*

e. The Dragons of Eden *by Carl Sagan*
f. Sophie's Choice *by William Styron*
g. Looking for Mr. Goodbar *by Judith Rossner*
h. Necessary Objects *by Lois Gould*
i. Trinity *by Leon Uris*
j. I'm Dancing as Fast as I Can *by Barbara Gordon*
k. Daniel Martin *by John Fowles*
l. Jonathan Livingston Seagull *by Richard Bach*
m. The Secret Life of Plants *by Peter Tompkins and Christopher Bird*
n. The Lives of a Cell *by Lewis Thomas*
o. Chesapeake *by James A. Michener*

(answers on page 228)

Movies 10

1. What was the last picture shown in *The Last Picture Show?*
2. This John Travolta–Olivia Newton-John musical was known as *Gummina* in France, *Brilliantino* in Italy, and *Vaselina* in Mexico. What was its American title?
3. In the movie *Where's Poppa?* where was Poppa?
4. What was the name of the film that Alvy Singer (Woody Allen) repeatedly went to see in *Annie Hall?*
5. Why did Dawn Davenport (Divine) stomp on all the presents and knock over the Christmas tree in *Female Trouble?*
6. What piece of classical music did Lieutenant Colonel Bill Kilgore (Robert Duvall) play while leading his helicopter bombing raid in *Apocalypse Now?*
7. In *Network*, name the revolutionary group that was hired by UBS to create acts of terrorism for its weekly TV show *The Mao Tse-tung Hour.*
8. What was the name of Sylvester Stallone's first movie?
9. How did *The Rose* (Bette Midler) respond when told at a truck-stop restaurant, "We don't serve hippies"?
10. Gloria Swanson ended a 22-year retirement to star in this, her last movie. (Given the caliber of the film, maybe she shouldn't have bothered.) She insisted on writing all of her own lines for this disaster film. Name it.
11. Who was Won Ton Ton, and what did he save?
12. What was made out of split-pea soup and oatmeal and made quite a splash on the movie screen?
13. He played Professor Kingsfield in both the movie and TV versions of *The Paper Chase*. Name him.
14. Out of what anthropological work did Playboy Productions make a movie?
15. Why did feminists complain that Bernardo Bertolucci's film *Last Tango in Paris* was sexist?

(answers on page 229)

Events 2

Once again, match the event with the year.

1970
1971
1972
1973
1974
1975
1976
1977
1978
1979

a. *Agnew resigns*
b. *Cambodians seize Mayaguez*
c. *Carter, Sadat, and Begin meet at Camp David*
d. *Burglars discovered at Watergate*
e. *Pope visits U.S., rides in popemobile*
f. *Kissinger visits China, paves way for Nixon*
g. *Outbreak of Legionnaire's Disease*
h. *Kent State shootings*
i. *Nixon pardoned, suffers terrible phlebitis*
j. *Vietnam draft evaders pardoned*

(answers on page 229)

Theater

1. The cast of this Broadway musical, which opened in 1971, had to fight its way into the theater past angry picketers every night. What was the play?
2. Name the off-Broadway lampoon of current events that featured John Belushi and Chevy Chase before they went on *Saturday Night Live* and became famous.
3. This work by Ntozake Shange was described as a "choreo-poem" in which seven black women used dance and poetry to tell their stories of love, rape, poverty, and self-searching. The play's name was also unusual. What was it?
4. Who acted cool at Rydell High School?
5. When did 13-year-old Andrea McArdle keep hoping the sun would come out?

Nathan Lee Morgan (Paul Winfield) and son David Lee (Kevin Hooks) watch apprehensively as the sheriff approaches in this 1972 movie, named after the dog pictured here. What was it called?

Answer:
Sounder

6. What was the name of Broadway's first—and last—disco musical, which was a $2 million failure in 1979?

7. This dramatist's *Travesties*, which came to New York in 1975, featured a debate between James Joyce and Vladimir Lenin on the merits of art. Name the playwright.

8. In *A Chorus Line*, 17 people were competing for how many openings in the chorus?

9. What version of the *Wizard of Oz*, starring a black cast, opened on Broadway in 1975 and produced the hit song "Ease on Down the Road"?

10. Name the Mark Medoff play that opened off-Broadway in 1973 and featured a lonely Western diner terrorized by a young tough.

11. Carol Channing starred in this musical—described by one reviewer as a "particularly tawdry retread" of her role in *Gentlemen Prefer Blondes*—which opened in Oklahoma City in 1973 and went on to play 17 cities. What was its name?

12. This Bob Fosse musical about the son of Charlemagne, starring John Rubinstein and Ben Vereen, became a big hit in 1972. What was it?

13. In *Sweeney Todd*, what happened to the demon barber's victims?

14. A musical version of which Shakespeare play won the Tony for best musical in 1972?

15. He may have been the greatest at boxing, but he wasn't necessarily great at acting. Name the off-Broadway play, starring Muhammad Ali, which failed in 1970.

(answers on page 229)

Space

1. What did NASA, in 1977, call "The first major structures in the solar system to be found since the discovery of Pluto in 1930"?

2. On July 17, 1975, U.S. and Soviet spaceships docked together in space, the first time that spacecraft built by different nations had done so. The American craft was part of the Apollo series. Name its Soviet counterpart.

3. In 1979 scientists discovered the first active volcanos outside of Earth.

Where were these volcanos located?
(Hint: They weren't on a planet.)

4. What was the number of the last U.S.
manned lunar flight of the decade?
Who was the last American to walk on
the moon?

5. On June 22, 1978, Pluto was found to
have a moon. What was it named, and
why?

6. Voyagers 1 and 2 each carried a gold-
coated copper phonograph record for
the listening pleasure of any extrater-
restrials who might come across the
spacecraft sometime in the future. Of
the following eight pieces of music,
which two were *not* included on the
Voyager records?

   a. *"Queen of Night" aria from* The
   Magic Flute *by Wolfgang
   Amadeus Mozart*
   b. *"Johnny B. Goode" by Chuck
   Berry*
   c. *"Liebestod" from* Tristan und
   Isolde *by Richard Wagner*
   d. *"Here Comes the Sun" by the
   Beatles*
   e. *Pygmy girls' initiation song*

   f. *Brandenberg Concerto No. 2 in
   F Major, First Movement, by Jo-
   hann Sebastian Bach*
   g. *Navajo night chant*
   h. *Symphony No. 5 in C Minor,
   First Movement, by Ludwig van
   Beethoven*

7. Name the first spacecraft to go into orbit around another planet. Name the
planet.

8. What was unusual about Apollo 13's
moon landing?

9. One of the main purposes of Vikings 1
and 2 was to search for evidence of life
on Mars. Did they find any?

10. In 1979 scientists were surprised when
Voyagers 1 and 2 discovered that
Jupiter had a physical feature in common with at least two other planets in
the solar system. What?

11. Name the first manned space station.

12. In October 1975, Soviet unmanned
spacecraft transmitted the first pictures
from the surface of another planet.
Which planet? (Give yourself bonus
points, or an honorary degree in astro-
physics, if you can name the spacecraft.)

13. Name the three astronauts involved in a scandal because they carried 398 unauthorized postal covers (i.e., stamped and canceled envelopes) with them to the moon for later private sale.
14. Why were the people of Australia upset at the U.S.—and especially NASA—in 1979?
15. Name the nuclear-powered Soviet satellite that crashed in northern Canada on January 24, 1978, scattering more than 100 pounds of radioactive debris over thousands of square miles.

(answers on page 230)

Quotes 5

Who said:

1. "In the forties, to get a girl you had to be a GI or a jock. In the fifties, to get a girl you had to be Jewish. In the sixties, to get a girl you had to be black. In the seventies, to get a girl you've got to be a girl."

    a. *Johnny Carson*
    b. *Steve Allen*
    c. *Mort Sahl*
    d. *J. Edgar Hoover*

2. "I love gay people. . . . But they are not a minority whose rights have to be protected. . . . If gays are granted rights, next we'll have to give rights to prostitutes and to people who sleep with Saint Bernards and to nail-biters."

    a. *Jerry Falwell*
    b. *Anita Bryant*
    c. *Tammy Faye Bakker*
    d. *Woody Allen*

3. "There's nothing wrong with going to bed with somebody of your own sex. . . . People should be very free with sex—they should draw the line at goats."

    a. *Elton John*
    b. *Truman Capote*
    c. *Gore Vidal*
    d. *Kermit the Frog*

To whom is Princess Leia (Carrie Fisher) registering her profound displeasure regarding the state of affairs in the empire? And while we're at it, what two actors shared the role of Darth Vader in *Star Wars*?

Answer:
Grand Moff Tarkin (Peter Cushing). Darth Vader's voice was that of James Earl Jones; his body belonged to David Prowse.

4. "Normal love isn't interesting. I assure you that it's incredibly boring."

    a. *Xaviera Hollander*
    b. *Roman Polanski*
    c. *Judy Chavez*
    d. *Roxanne Pulitzer*

5. "I can do anything. One of these days I'll be so complete I won't be a human. I'll be a god."

    a. *Maharaj Ji*
    b. *Werner Erhard*
    c. *Sun Myung Moon*
    d. *John Denver*

6. "I would have made a good pope."

    a. *Henry Kissinger*
    b. *Richard Nixon*
    c. *Jimmy Carter*
    d. *Charlton Heston*

7. "If men could get pregnant, abortion would be a sacrament."

    a. *Ti-Grace Atkinson*
    b. *Gloria Steinem*
    c. *Florynce Kennedy*
    d. *Daniel Berrigan*

8. "We have lived through the era when happiness was a warm puppy, and the era when happiness was a dry martini, and now we have come to the era when happiness is 'knowing what your uterus looks like.'"

    a. *Nora Ephron*
    b. *Lily Tomlin*
    c. *Gilda Radner*
    d. *David Reuben*

9. "Women have childbearing equipment. For them to choose not to use the equipment is no more blocking what is instinctive than it is for a man who, muscles or no, chooses not to be a weightlifter."

    a. *Ellen Peck*
    b. *Betty Rollin*
    c. *Benjamin Spock*
    d. *Arnold Schwarzenegger*

10. "Now there is one outstanding important fact regarding Spaceship Earth,
and that is that no instruction book
came with it."

    a. David Brower
    b. R. Buckminster Fuller
    c. Jerry Brown
    d. Leonard Nimoy

11. "We have probed the earth, excavated
it, burned it, ripped things from it,
buried things in it. . . . That does not fit
my definition of a good tenant. If we
were here on a month-to-month basis,
we would have been evicted long
ago."

    a. Barry Commoner
    b. Rose Bird
    c. David Brower
    d. Euell Gibbons

12. "Obviously, the answer to oil spills is to
paper-train the tankers."

    a. Dick Cavett
    b. Ralph Nader
    c. Ronald Reagan
    d. King Faisal

13. "The mother of the year should be a
sterilized woman with two adopted
children."

    a. R. Buckminster Fuller
    b. Paul Ehrlich
    c. Jane Fonda
    d. Mao Tse-Tung

14. "If I'm saving the whale, why am I eating tuna fish?"

    a. Jacques Cousteau
    b. Jerry Brown
    c. Ram Dass
    d. Julia Child

15. "People in nutrition get the idea that
they are going to live to be a hundred
and fifty. And they never do."

    a. Nathan Pritikin
    b. Adelle Davis
    c. J. I. Rodale
    d. Herman Tarnower

(answers on page 231)

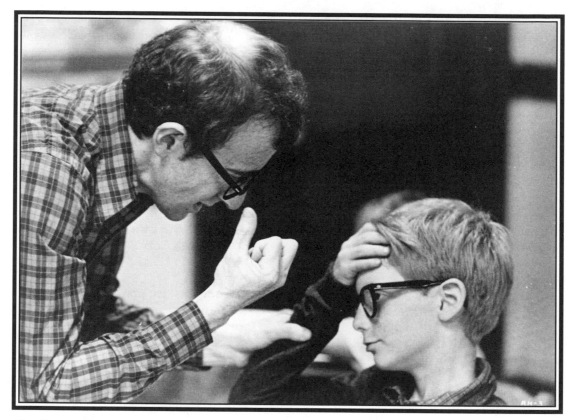

Alvy Singer (Woody Allen) talks to himself as a boy in *Annie Hall*. What actor played the young Alvy Singer?

Books 2

1. This author "helped" Howard Hughes write his autobiography while helping himself to $650,000 in advance money, but he was later forced to admit it was all a fraud when the billionaire recluse denied ever having met him. Name the author.

2. Two American authors won the Nobel Prize for Literature during the '70s. Name them.

3. When mystery writer Agatha Christie died in 1976, she left a book to be published posthumously. It featured her female sleuth, Miss Marple. Name it.

4. Speaking of posthumous publications, Ernest Hemingway left a draft of a book he'd written years before, which was finally published in 1970 with only minor editing. Some said it was wonderful, Hemingway returned to his old form; others said it could have used that final reworking. Name this book.

5. Fantasy writer J. R. R. Tolkien also had a book published posthumously during the '70s. This book, which the author had considered his most important work, formed the background of The Hobbit and The Lord of the Rings trilogy. What was it called?

6. Who was *The Happy Hooker?*

7. What women's health book was permanently removed from school libraries in Helena, Montana, after the state attorney general's office wrote in 1978 that "any person distributing it to a child under the age of 16 could be subject to criminal charges"?

8. Where was *Ecotopia?*

9. Why was no Pulitzer Prize awarded for fiction in 1973?

10. Who wrote the 1976 novel *The Canfield Decision?*

11. In his book *The 100: A Ranking of the Most Influential Persons in History,* whom did author Michael Hart put at the top of his list?

12. This 1946 best-seller was revised in 1976 to keep up with changing times. Besides now referring to babies as "she" as well as "he," the book also addressed the importance of the father's role in child-rearing and the situation of the working mother. Gone from this updated edition were such gems as "Women are usually more patient in

working at unexciting repetitive tasks."
Name the book.

13. Kurt Vonnegut wrote two Kilgore Trout novels during the '70s. Name them.

14. This tell-all book, written by two of Elvis Presley's former bodyguards with some help from a tabloid editor, was published two weeks before the entertainer died. Depicting Elvis as a fat, drugged-out control freak with a penchant for the supernatural, it sold more than three million copies. What was it called?

15. Name the best-selling book written by baseball pitcher James Bouton that gave the dish on baseball players and led to baseball commissioner Bowie Kuhn warning Bouton "against future writings of this kind."

(answers on page 231)

Numbers—Economics

Match the correct number to each item.

1. The number of days that President Nixon froze wages and prices starting August 15, 1971

2. The percentage of the U.S. auto market controlled by domestic automakers in 1972

3. The cost, in dollars, of a mantra from a Transcendental Meditation center in 1975

4. The number of pennies it took to send a first-class letter in 1976

5. The retail price, in dollars, of the first truly portable calculator, a 2.5-pound model introduced by Texas Instruments in 1971

6. The amount, in dollars, of the capital with which Steven Jobs and Stephen Wozniak started Apple Computer in 1976

7. The number of pennies needed to buy a gallon of gas on Labor Day weekend 1977

8. The number of pennies needed to buy a gallon of gas two years later

9. The annual percentage inflation rate in 1979

10. The approximate number of times Jimmy Carter said he prayed every day

    a. 13
    b. 65
    c. 1,300
    d. 90
    e. 125
    f. 25
    g. 18
    h. 150
    i. 97
    j. 86

(answers on page 232)

Movies 11

1. What color soap did Annie Hall use to wash her face?
2. This politically correct movie featured a one-armed child who played guitar with his hook and who was later blown away when the "progressive" school he attended was attacked by the National Guard. Name the film.
3. What was the X-rated parody of *Flash Gordon* called?
4. How did the auto racers earn points in the cult film *Death Race 2000*?
5. This movie had no human actors, only birds. Name it.
6. What was Vito Corleone better known as?
7. Name Bruce Lee's first kung fu movie.
8. Roy Rogers made a comeback in this 1975 film, his first movie in 22 years. Name it.
9. In what movie did Merv Griffin sing the national anthem at the start of the "Championship X" football game?
10. George Lucas's first feature film was a longer version of a short he'd made while a student at USC. Name it.
11. Who were the Oompa-Loompas?
12. By what name was the reincarnated Audrey Rose known in her new life?
13. Who were the Glory Riders?
14. Johnny Cash called this movie, for which he produced and wrote eight songs and in which he and his wife June Carter Cash starred, "my life's proudest work. It's the reason I'm on this earth." Name it.
15. What was Project Wildfire?

(answers on page 232)

Who Did What? 3

1. Robert Pearson
2. Marcel Lefebvre
3. Crystal Lee Sutton
4. Leonard Peltier
5. Danny McCoy
6. Cheryl Browne
7. Bernard Shaw
8. Janet Guthrie
9. Pierre Laporte
10. Rodney Allen Rippy
11. Elaine Noble
12. Nancy Maginnes
13. Maggie Kuhn
14. Philippe Petit
15. Dwight Elliott Stone

a. *First black to compete in Miss America pageant*
b. *Quebec minister of labour kidnapped and murdered by French-Canadian separatists*
c. *Man who married Patty Hearst*
d. *High-wire artist who illegally walked between World Trade Centers in 1974*
e. *Woman who married Henry Kissinger*
f. *Union organizer upon whose efforts Norma Rae was based*
g. *Founder of "Uglies Unlimited," a group formed to fight discrimination against ugly people*
h. *First openly lesbian state legislator*
i. *Founder of the Gray Panthers*
j. *Army private who stole helicopter and landed it on White House lawn*
k. *Last U.S. draftee (who, incidentally, tried to dodge)*
l. *First woman to drive in the Indy 500*
m. *American Indian Movement leader convicted of murdering two FBI agents in South Dakota gun battle*
n. *Child actor famous for his hamburger commercials*
o. *Catholic archbishop who defied the Vatican*

(answers on page 233)

Trends 3

1. By 1972 sales of this breakfast-food product were doubling every 60 to 90 days. What was it?
2. Who broke Farrah Fawcett-Majors' poster sales record?
3. The movie *Rocky* was considered responsible for a phenomenal increase in sales of this athletic product: One Los Angeles manufacturer was churning out 50,000 per month and couldn't keep up. What was it?
4. What was a Vegimel?
5. In 1975 this magazine decided to avoid frontal nudity and reduce the use of four-letter words in an effort to gain respectability. Name it.
6. Arthur Janov's 1971 best-seller bore the name of his brand of psychotherapy, which became a rage during the '70s and cause for five more books. What was the first book's title?
7. California's Proposition 13 was a shot heard 'round the world, or at least around the country. What two men spearheaded the successful 1978 tax-cutting initiative?
8. Whose fundamental truth, available during weekend lectures costing $300, was "What is, is; what isn't, isn't"?
9. There was Mother's Day, there was Father's Day, and in the '70s advocates of the right not to have children tried to initiate what holiday?
10. During the mid-'70s a number of wrinkle-conscious Los Angeles women began using this product on their faces at night, even though it was intended for a different part of the body and dermatologists warned against it. What was it?
11. Sales of these toys were up 44 percent in 1977, and related injuries were up 161 percent, dude. What were they?
12. In 1978 McDonald's had to fight nasty rumors that its hamburgers contained what?
13. During the '70s, where could women finally go to see a bunch of sweaty, naked men?
14. The first gay doll was introduced in 1978 by Gizmo Development, a New York firm. Barbie had Ken; but if Ken were bi, what would the name of his "friend" be?
15. "To everything there is a season," the commercial began. "There is a right time

for children . . . when they are wanted."
So began the first televised ad for
what, on the San Jose, California, ABC
affiliate in August 1975?

(answers on page 233)

Music 7

1. This group put out albums in the early
   '70s with such titles as *Free Your Mind
   and Your Ass Will Follow, America Eats
   Its Young,* and *Cosmic Slop.* Name the
   group.
2. In 1975 Michael Murphy gave us the
   semi-heartwrenching ballad of a horse
   that got lost when a dreaded "killing
   frost" developed. What was the name
   of that poor horse?
3. Why did Ravi Shankar, George Harrison, Ringo Starr, Eric Clapton, Leon
   Russell, and others gather for a two-
   day concert at Madison Square Gar-
   den in 1971?
4. Thanks in large part to the score for the
   movie *The Sting,* ragtime music under-
   went a revival in 1973–74. This led to
   renewed fame for what long-dead
   composer? And what was the name of
   his forgotten opera that was staged on
   Broadway in 1975?
5. Their first album, *Briefcase Full of
   Blues,* astonished everyone at Atlantic
   Records by going platinum within
   three weeks. Who were they?
6. This group started out in gospel but
   ended up country with the 1977 hit
   "Y'all Come Back Saloon." Who were
   they?
7. What national leader banned the
   broadcast of music over radio and TV
   in 1979, saying it "stupefies persons listening to it and makes their brains in-
   active and frivolous"?
8. He won the People's Choice Award for
   top male singer three times in the late
   '70s. Name him.
9. Why were six record companies and 16
   people indicted on June 24, 1975?
10. Who was the Divine Miss M? And
    in 1972–73, what then-unknown pi-
    anist/arranger helped put together the
    revue that moved her from singing at
    gay bathhouses in New York to the na-
    tional stage?

11. What Jamaican movie helped introduce Americans to the reggae beat in 1973?
12. Why did Minnie Pearl break down and cry on the stage of the Grand Ole Opry on March 26, 1974?
13. In 1975 this 26-year-old performer was given a record-breaking $13-million recording contract by Motown Records. Who was he?
14. Name the jazz guitarist who rose to the top of the pop charts in 1976 with his album *Breezin'* and his hit single "This Masquerade."
15. This 1974 Ray Stevens hit was named after the latest national fad. What was it?

(answers on page 234)

True Or False? 4

Eight of the following 10 items are true. Can you ferret out the two fakes?

1. Perceived as washed up after the cancellation of *Dan August*, Burt Reynolds appeared as a bachelor on *The Dating Game*—and wasn't chosen.
2. While Patty Hearst was in jail on bank robbery charges in San Francisco in 1976, she received a letter inviting her to take out a credit card.
3. Alabama Governor George Wallace had a wheelchair race with Raymond Burr on the set of *Ironside* and won.
4. Robert H. Simpson of Sacramento, California, celebrated his 93rd birthday on July 8, 1973, with his 234th arrest for picketing the California State Capitol. He was arrested while protesting an antipicketing statute known as the Simpson Law, which had been specifically passed to prevent him from picketing.
5. In 1970 scientists found 17 amino acids, six of which are usually present in living cells on Earth, in a meteorite that had crashed in Australia.
6. When *The Good News Paper* went out of business in 1972, it didn't report on its own demise because that would have been bad news.
7. Eccentric heiress Gwendolyn Pendergast purchased the small town of Charlene, Georgia, in 1971 and pro-

ceeded to rename the streets after her cats, thus running afoul of the county planning commission, which objected to such names as "Mr. Whiskers Boulevard" and "Fuzzbutton Circle."

8. The 1976 Republican platform supported ratification of the Equal Rights Amendment.

9. Seventy-three-year-old Cincinnati judge Fred Cramer decided to get "with it" in 1977 by wearing a robe made of blue denim, which had a loop attached to the side for carrying his gavel.

10. Nixon Interior Secretary Walter Hickel wanted to make Earth Day a national holiday.

(answers on page 234)

TV 12

1. What was Radar O'Reilly's real first name?
2. Why did Kojak suck lollipops?
3. Maude Findlay ran through three housekeepers during the time that *Maude* was on the air. Who were they?
4. Tony Baretta had a pet. What was it, and what was its name?
5. Although *Mork & Mindy* was responsible for making Robin Williams a star, it was not his first TV series. What was?
6. Where could you watch "Pigs in Space"?
7. Name the crime reporter for Chicago's Independent News Service who covered such stories as a vampire murdering young women in Las Vegas, a succubus preying on students on a college campus, and the original Jack the Ripper attacking women in Chicago—but whose stories never saw print because his editor never believed him.
8. What was building superintendent Schneider's first name on *One Day at a Time*?
9. Who actually did the magic tricks that Bill Bixby ostensibly performed on *The Magician*?
10. What was the name of the family in *Family*?
11. Who was the announcer on *The Midnight Special*?

12. Almost everyone associates the TV role of Perry Mason with Raymond Burr, but during the '70s, while Burr was playing in *Ironside*, someone else starred as Perry Mason. Who?
13. What was the name of the corner bar that Archie Bunker frequented (and later bought)?
14. For what TV show was John Philip Sousa's "Liberty Bell March" the theme song?
15. Who worked at Otto's Auto Orphanage?

(answers on page 234)

Stranger Than Fiction

Watergate may have been painful for the country, but it was a boon for the publishing industry. Match each book below with the Watergate-related author who wrote it.

1. *The Right and the Power*
2. *The Ends of Power*
3. *From Power to Peace*
4. *Chief Counsel*
5. *Born Again*
6. *Blind Ambition*
7. *Out of Control*
8. *Counterfeit Kill*
9. *To Set the Record Straight*
10. *The Company*

   a. John Ehrlichman
   b. Chuck Colson
   c. John Dean
   d. Leon Jaworski
   e. Jeb Stuart Magruder
   f. H. R. Haldeman
   g. Samuel Dash
   h. G. Gordon Liddy
   i. E. Howard Hunt
   j. John Sirica

(answers on page 235)

Women 5

1. Name the Mormon woman excommunicated by her church for her outspoken support of the Equal Rights Amendment.
2. What occurred in Houston in November 1977 that attracted Betty Ford, Rosalynn Carter, Lady Bird Johnson, and thousands of other women?
3. Although she was more famous under a pseudonym, Norma McCorvey was instrumental in furthering the cause of reproductive freedom for women during the '70s. By what name was she better known?
4. In March 1979, what piece of clothing did Iranian women demonstrate against being forced to wear?
5. This U.S. representative could be considered the modern-day "Mother of the ERA" for her work in getting the proposed amendment passed in Congress, where it had languished for 20 years. Who was she?
6. Why were feminists upset when Jackie Onassis took a job at Viking Press for $10,000 in 1975?
7. Two women were named Sportswoman of the Year by *Sports Illustrated* during the '70s—one by herself and one sharing the title. Who were they?
8. In 1977 Dane County, Wisconsin, judge Archie Simonson wound up in a recall election because he said that this crime was "normal," thus angering many of his constituents. What crime was he referring to?
9. What did the feminist organization WITCH stand for?
10. Who wrote, "A Total Woman caters to her man's special quirks, whether it be in salads, sex or sports"?
11. What did five women have to do at American Cyanamid Company's West Virginia plant in 1978 to keep their jobs?
12. Who was the first black woman to run for president?
13. Why did two Austin, Texas, Girl Scout leaders burn their uniforms in 1977?

"You're crazy, weird, exasperating," Mindy
once said to Mork. "I can't help it," he replied,
"I'm _____ ."
What?

a. an Orkan
b. your roommate
c. a Libran
d. on drugs

Answer:
c

14. In 1975, for the first time in U.S. history, more women than men did something. What?
15. What double standard did young mother Ida Phillips run up against when she applied for a job at the Martin Marietta Corporation?

(answers on page 235)

News 5

1. Arthritic and almost toothless, this elderly lion became a sexual celebrity in 1971 when he was put out to pasture among a pride of 12 hard-to-please lionesses at Southern California's Lion Country Safari and unexpectedly turned out to be an incredible kitty stud. This sensuous lion was even named "Father of the Year" in a congressional resolution. What was his name?
2. Lion Country Safari, sensing further opportunities for publicity, named this human its "Sensuous Man of the Year" for 1972. What was *his* name?
3. To what was Jimmy Carter referring when he said, "There are many things in life that are not fair"?
4. This nation's first satellite was launched on April 24, 1970, and, until it went dead a month later, circled the globe bursting out in the revolutionary song "The East Is Red." What country brought music to the spheres?
5. In 1973 Arizona, known for its clean air, became the first state to do what?
6. The Trilateral Commission was formed in the mid-'70s to foster political and economic cooperation between the U.S., Japan, and Western Europe. Conspiracy theorists said that it was a shadow government. Which two of the following were *not* members?

> *David Rockefeller*
> *Zbigniew Brzezinski*
> *Gerald Ford*
> *John Anderson*
> *George Bush*
> *Jimmy Carter*
> *Ronald Reagan*
> *Walter Mondale*
> *Cyrus Vance*
> *Warren Christopher*

Andrew Young
Caspar Weinberger
Prince Charles
Lane Kirkland
Henry Kissinger
Baron Edmond de Rothschild

7. In the late '70s, what did federal drug agents spray on the U.S. marijuana crop?

8. In what country did throwing hand grenades become a recognized sport, with 36 million people participating?

9. In 1972 scientists at the University of Chicago determined that this was 24 hours long. What?

10. First they lived on dried fruit and candy, then they made a soup of lichens. When that ran out, what did the 16 survivors of a 1972 plane crash in the Andes Mountains do for food while awaiting rescue?

11. In 1979 the House Select Committee on Assassinations took issue with two major conclusions of the Warren Commission regarding the shooting of President John F. Kennedy. What were they?

12. This man was the only person to serve in the cabinets of all three presidents during the '70s. Who was he and what posts did he fill?

13. Why were the three Soyuz 11 cosmonauts found strapped dead in their seats when their spacecraft landed, intact, in 1971?

14. On August 6, 1970, Paolo Soleri began construction of his ecology-friendly city of the future, located 70 miles north of Phoenix. What was it called?

15. A fatal outbreak of botulism in the early '70s was attributed to what brand of canned vichyssoise?

(answers on page 236)

Super Bowls

Ah, those '70s Super Bowls. The Pittsburgh Steelers. The Miami Dolphins. The Dallas Cowboys. The Minnesota Vikings. The Pittsburgh Steelers. The Miami Dolphins. The Dallas Cowboys ... It seemed like the same teams were playing over and over, which they pretty much were. Below, in Column A, are the years and the scores. In Column B are the winners, jumbled up of course. In Column C are the losers, also jumbled. Match the right winner and the right loser to the right year.

A

1.	1970	23–7
2.	1971	16–13
3.	1972	24–3
4.	1973	14–7
5.	1974	24–7
6.	1975	16–6
7.	1976	21–17
8.	1977	32–14
9.	1978	27–10
10.	1979	35–31

B

Pittsburgh Steelers
Pittsburgh Steelers
Pittsburgh Steelers
Miami Dolphins
Miami Dolphins
Dallas Cowboys
Dallas Cowboys
Oakland Raiders
Kansas City Chiefs
Baltimore Colts

C

Minnesota Vikings
Minnesota Vikings
Minnesota Vikings
Minnesota Vikings
Miami Dolphins
Dallas Cowboys
Dallas Cowboys
Dallas Cowboys
Denver Broncos
Washington Redskins

(answers on page 237)

People 7

1. Who said, "Less is more"?
2. Who said, "Small is beautiful"?
3. Who said, "Let's get small"?
4. This rock star and fellow Finch College graduate was invited when Tricia Nixon hosted a tea party for college alumni in April 1970, but she didn't get past the White House gate. Who was she and why?
5. Why did a group of Catholic laymen urge that U.S. Supreme Court Justice William Brennan be excommunicated from the church?
6. The term "skyjacker" was coined in 1971 when a man boarded a plane with a briefcase, claimed it contained a bomb, collected $200,000, and parachuted out somewhere over the Pacific Northwest. Authorities never found him. Who was he?
7. In 1978 this TV actor was found clubbed to death in a Scottsdale, Arizona, motel room where he had been filming himself in sexual acts with various women. Name him.
8. Which president appeared on the stage of the Grand Ole Opry?
9. On July 2, 1979, Chicago DJ Steve Dahl dynamited something in the middle of Comiskey Park between games of a White Sox–Detroit Lions doubleheader. A small riot ensued, and the field was so damaged that the White Sox had to forfeit the second game. What had Dahl blown up?
10. What famous American said, "I don't laugh at people any more when they say they've seen UFO's, because I've seen one myself"?
11. Two of the Andrews Sisters rode the '40s nostalgia boom to Broadway in 1974 in a production of what play?
12. What was unusual about accused rapist William Milligan's defense in December 1978, which led to a verdict of not guilty by reason of insanity?
13. In 1972 and 1973, this individual was voted the most hated person in history by visitors to Madame Tussaud's waxworks museum in London, beating out Adolf Hitler, Jack the Ripper, and Satan. Who had this dubious honor?
14. Of what type of craft was Jan Tiura the first female skipper?

15. In Secret Service parlance, who were "Lockmaster," "Lotus Path," and "Lemondrop"?

(answers on page 237)

Movies 12

1. In this, John Wayne's last film, he played John Bernard Books, an aging gunfighter dying of cancer. At the time, Wayne really had cancer, and he died of it three years later. Name the film.
2. What 1977 film did French director Francois Truffaut appear in but not direct, because, he said, he wanted the experience of acting in someone else's movie?
3. At the end of *Blazing Saddles*, Hedley Lamarr (Harvey Korman) stopped at the theater's candy counter to buy something. What?
4. Yes, the environment became trendy during the '70s. Even Godzilla went earth-friendly in 1972 in a film in which he actually *saved* Tokyo from an environmental menace, although a few flicks of the old tail may have knocked down a building or two in the process. Name the film.
5. This 1975 musical, which featured Cybill Shepherd, Burt Reynolds, and Madeline Kahn bumbling their way through 16 Cole Porter songs, was so bad that Reynolds later said, "I think we bombed." What was it called?
6. This porno film became famous because it supposedly climaxed with footage of the real murder and dismemberment of its script girl—but it was actually all a hoax. Name the film.
7. What was the name of the orangutan in *Every Which Way But Loose*?
8. In *Monty Python and the Holy Grail*, in order to gain permission to cross the Bridge of Death, Sir Lancelot (John Cleese) had to answer three questions: "What is your name? What is your quest? What is your favorite color?" What were the three questions that Sir Robin (Eric Idle) had to answer?
9. Name the "hit creature" in the cantina in *Star Wars*.
10. What former sports figure played *The Last Rebel*?

11. Donald Sutherland played Jesus in this antiwar film about a soldier who had no legs, arms, or face. Name it.
12. Who, during the gunfighter phase of his very eventful life, was known as the "Soda Pop Kid"?
13. What monster movie did seven-foot, two-inch African Masai tribesman Bolaji Badejo star in?
14. In *Bite the Bullet*, how much did the *Western Press* give the winner of the horse race?
15. This film, about a wealthy Greek man who married the widow of a murdered Irish Catholic president (whose younger brother just happened to have been attorney general), had this disclaimer: "The characters in this film are purely fictitious and any resemblance to persons living or dead is purely coincidental." Name this purely fictitious picture.

(answers on page 237)

Songs 4

From these first lines, name the songs and the people who performed them.

1. "L.A.'s fine, the sun shines most of the time and the feelin' is lay back."
2. "L.A. proved too much for the man, so he's leavin' the life he's come to know."
3. "I heard he had a good song, I heard he had a style."
4. "I need you, baby, like a dog needs a bone."
5. "I rode my bicycle past your window last night."
6. "Time keeps on slippin', slippin', slippin'."
7. "I'm sleepin' and right in the middle of a good dream."
8. "They get up ev'ry mornin' from the 'larm clock warnin', take the eight fifteen into the city."
9. "If you wake up and don't want to smile."
10. "It's nine o'clock on a Saturday, the regular crowd shuffles in."
11. "I've been alive forever and I wrote the very first song."

12. "I've been walkin' these streets so long, singin' the same old song."
13. "I'm comin' home, I've done my time."
14. "Sittin' in the classroom, thinkin' it's a drag."
15. "If my words did glow, with the gold of sunshine."

(answers on page 238)

TV—Killer Questions

Do you still recall *Far Out Space Nuts* with a certain fondness? Has life lost its luster since *Grandpa Goes to Washington* was canceled? Then this section may be for you.

1. The Hudson Brothers had three separate TV programs during the 1970s. What were the names of the shows? For that matter, what were the names of the Hudson Brothers?
2. Name the short-lived, hour-long prime-time variety program that was hosted by two life-sized puppets.
3. Besides the Captain and Tennille, who were the only other regulars on *The Captain and Tennille?*
4. In 1978 the movie *National Lampoon's Animal House* was a big success. In early 1979 all three networks came up with knockoffs. Name the shows.
5. Who was Abraham Lincoln Imhook?
6. Despite the furor over Murphy Brown's decision to become an unwed mother, this wasn't a new issue for TV. In 1979—nearly a decade and a half earlier—CBS ran a show that featured a pregnant, unwed woman who decided not to marry the father of her child. What was the name of that show?
7. Who was Cruncher?
8. On what program was Garrett Morris a regular before *Saturday Night Live?*
9. The father starred in the movie; his daughter was a regular on the TV remake by the same name. Who were they, and what was the movie/TV show called?
10. Who was Mrs. Miskel Spillman?
11. Although Paul Shaffer is famous today as the leader of the CBS Orchestra, in the '70s he starred in a short-lived comedy series. What was it?

12. This summer 1977 musical variety show was hosted by a 12-year-old drummer and his 13-year-old piano-playing brother. Who were they, and what was the name of the show?

13. This actress was originally slated to play the mother on *Eight Is Enough* but died after only four episodes had been taped. For the rest of that season she was written as being "away," and in the following season Tom Bradford had become a widower. Who was she?

14. What was the name of the syndicated show that reversed male-female roles and featured a society where women were executives and men were secretaries and homemakers?

15. You probably remember that Andy Griffith played a small-town sheriff during the 1960s on *The Andy Griffith Show*. But do you remember the name of the '70s show on which he played a small-town sheriff, and which only lasted for two episodes?

(answers on page 238)

'70s Graduate Exam

We've saved some of the best, or at least the most impossible, for last.

1. Name the four members of Abba.
2. On a roll? OK, name the Gang of Four.
3. "I'd Like to Teach the World to Sing" became famous as a Coca-Cola commercial in 1972. A year earlier, before Coke reworked it, it was just another song by just another British group. What was the group, and what was the song originally called?
4. Archibald Cox and Leon Jaworski were the first and second Watergate special prosecutors. Who were the third and fourth?
5. What '70s event was the busiest day ever for FTD florists?
6. Who was Manolo Sanchez?
7. When Hank Aaron retired in 1976, he left a lifetime record of 755 home runs. Who broke that record one year later by hitting his 756th home run? (Hint: You might want to think over the roster of the Yomiuri Giants.)
8. Whose Mercedes bore the license plate "SO WUT"?

9. Though not a vice president, this man was a heartbeat away from the presidency twice during the 1970s. Name him.
10. What famous fugitive from Britain's "great train robbery" collaborated with the Sex Pistols on the song "The Biggest Blow—A Punk Prayer"?
11. Who was Mr. Muggs?
12. In 1972 China gave us two giant pandas, Hsing-Hsing and Ling-Ling. What did we give China, and what were their names?
13. Who was the last president of South Vietnam?
14. Who was held in Detention Block AA-23?
15. What did the Symbionese Liberation Army adopt as its theme song (yes, theme song)?

(answers on page 239)

Answers

'70s 1-A

1. President Nixon
2. The Committee to Re-Elect the President
3. Remulak
4. France
5. Solving the energy crisis, according to President Carter
6. The character played by John Travolta in *Saturday Night Fever*
7. Billie Jean King defeated Bobby Riggs (6–4, 6–3, 6–3) in 1973 at the Houston Astrodome.
8. "We are Devo."
9. Nelson Rockefeller
10. Tom Wolfe, in a 1976 essay

People 1

1. Urban guerrilla
2. The four students killed at Kent State
3. Ruth Carter Stapleton (Jimmy Carter's evangelical sister)
4. "Protector"
5. Henry Kissinger

6. Astrological incompatability. "A Taurus and a Leo is like two sticks of dynamite," he said.
7. Gary Mark Gilmore
8. The face of Jesus
9. Margaret Trudeau, in 1977
10. Pittsburgh Steelers linebacker Jack Lambert
11. Charlie Chaplin's
12. California Governor Jerry Brown
13. Hiding in the jungle on Guam. Fearing execution if he gave himself up and not aware that the war had ended, Yokoi lived on rats, snails, frogs, nuts, mangoes, and papayas, and fashioned his clothing out of bark and roots. Ten months after his discovery in 1972 he married a war widow; the couple planned to honeymoon on Guam.
14. Ghana
15. Jennie Eisenhower. She was Richard and Pat Nixon's first grandchild.

True or False? 1

Items 7 and 10 are false.

TV 1

1. Farrah Fawcett-Majors, Kate Jackson, Jaclyn Smith, Cheryl Ladd, and Shelley Hack. (The last Angel, Tanya Roberts, starred during the 1980–81 season.)
2. Fawcett-Majors played Jill Munroe, Jackson played Sabrina Duncan, Smith played Kelly Garrett, Ladd played Kris Munroe, and Hack played Tiffany Welles.
3. Mary Hartman's grandfather, Raymond Larkin, who was known for his tendency to expose himself in public, on *Mary Hartman, Mary Hartman*
4. Twinkies, on *All in the Family*
5. John Boy Walton, on *The Waltons*
6. $3,000, which he said they could divide up any way they wanted. A few weeks later he reappeared and sweetened the pot to $3,200.
7. Warren Weber
8. "Nanu, nanu," according to Mork, on *Mork & Mindy*
9. *The Dick Cavett Show*
10. The S.W.A.T. team, on *S.W.A.T.*
11. The "mystical, magical" nanny on *Nanny and the Professor*
12. *Joe Forrester*
13. This mixed-marriage sitcom, in which an Irish Catholic woman married a Jewish man, drew protests from religious, primarily Jewish, groups, so CBS decided to cancel it. (The show's stars, Meredith Baxter and David Birney, were later married in real life.)
14. Ben
15. The Louds

Songs 1

1. "Stairway to Heaven" by Led Zeppelin
2. "American Pie" by Don McLean
3. "Le Freak" by Chic
4. "Rocky Mountain High" by John Denver
5. "Rock and Roll Hoochie Koo" by Rick Derringer
6. "Me and Julio Down by the Schoolyard" by Paul Simon
7. "Blinded by the Light" by Bruce Springsteen
8. "Peace Train" by Cat Stevens
9. "It's Only Rock 'n' Roll" by the Rolling Stones
10. "Rainy Days and Mondays" by the Carpenters

11. "Lean on Me" by Bill Withers
12. "Rock the Boat" by Hues Corporation
13. "Bad, Bad Leroy Brown" by Jim Croce
14. "In the Navy" by the Village People
15. "Margaritaville" by Jimmy Buffet

Women 1

1. Sarah Weddington
2. 46. Only Alaska, Hawaii, New York, and Washington were unaffected.
3. Although Hughes admitted that she had murdered her husband, Mickey, by setting fire to the bedroom while he slept, a jury acquitted her in 1977 after testimony that he had beaten her for more than a decade.
4. 5–2, Bobby Riggs over Billie Jean King
5. NOW had urged organizations and groups that supported the ERA not to hold conventions and meetings in unratified states. Missouri, which had not passed the ERA, objected and sued. In 1979 a U.S. District Court upheld NOW's right to boycott.
6. Antonia Brico
7. The attempted rape of an 8-year-old girl. The station received many complaints and pulled Antoine from the air.
8. In an effort to call attention to the problem of rape, thousands of women across the country marched one evening in 1977 to show their solidarity and right to safely walk the streets at night.
9. They wanted "an immediate stop to the publication of articles that are irrelevant, unstimulating, and demeaning to the women of America" and won the right to publish a special insert, which appeared in the August 1970 issue. The *Journal* had been chosen, a protester said, because it had refused to run articles on women's liberation and had depicted women as "totally passive, ever-suffering second-class citizens."
10. 1975
11. Their wives had asked them to.
12. Jane Byrne, in February 1979, with 82.5 percent of the vote
13. It let them join its marching band.
14. They burned all but the bra. The diploma was burned because the women felt that the University of California (one campus of which is located in Berkeley) failed to teach women

anything relevant to their situation in society; the book by Norman Mailer was burned because of his professed male chauvinism; and *Good Housekeeping*'s list was burned because the women on it were identified by their husbands' names only.

15. The First Women's Bank

News 1

1. Comet Kohoutek
2. Military reservists
3. He shot George Wallace at a 1972 campaign rally in Laurel, Maryland.
4. It was indicted for deaths resulting from the poorly designed gas tank of the Ford Pinto, which tended to explode in rear-end collisions. Despite evidence that the company knew of the defect in advance, Ford was acquitted.
5. Cyanide and Flavour-Aide
6. "It was an act of God," said Chairman Charles F. Luce.
7. It was inadvertently bombed by the Israeli Air Force during the 1973 Yom Kippur War.
8. He was the head of the Symbionese Liberation Army, which kidnapped Patty Hearst. Cinque was an alias; his real name was Donald DeFreeze.
9. They baked a 60-square-foot cherry pie, of course.
10. Vice President Spiro Agnew, who pleaded *nolo contendere* (no contest) to charges of tax evasion and resigned October 10, 1973
11. The American Indian Movement
12. Bert Lance
13. The death penalty, largely due to the arbitrary and discriminatory way in which some states then imposed it. The court reversed itself in 1976 after the arrival of more conservative appointees and after 35 states and the federal government changed their laws to overcome the court's objections.
14. The Teton Dam
15. Gold

Quotes 1

1. d
2. d
3. c
4. a
5. b
6. d
7. d
8. b
9. d
10. a
11. c
12. b
13. c
14. c
15. a

Music 1

1. "You Light Up My Life" by Debbie Boone
2. British punk rockers Ian Dury, Chaz Jankel, and Davey Payne, later known as Ian Dury and the Blockheads
3. David Cassidy. He also said he was tired of being a Partridge.
4. "Mother and Child Reunion," in 1972

5. Sex Pistol Sid Vicious, who died of a heroin overdose a few months after stabbing Spungen, his girlfriend, in 1978
6. Many people objected to the image of a seductively smiling, bound and beaten woman used for cover art and advertising for the Rolling Stones' *Black and Blue* album. The boycott of Warner Brothers, Elektra/Asylum, and Atlantic Records was called off when the parent company agreed to "strongly discourage the use of images of physical and sexual violence against women" in advertising and album covers.
7. Johnny Rodriguez
8. The usual amount of male ejaculation is 9 cc.
9. Bruce Springsteen
10. Jerry Lee Lewis. He was arrested for public intoxication.
11. Frank Sinatra
12. Kiss
13. George Harrison; "My Sweet Lord"
14. "Puppy Love," sung by Donny Osmond. Morgan had been playing it as a comment on the state of popular music.
15. d

Numbers—Culture

1. f or g
2. i
3. j
4. d or e
5. a
6. d or e
7. b
8. c
9. f or g
10. h

Sports 1

1. 755
2. The man who, in 1979 at a speed of 739.666 mph, first broke the sound barrier on land in his car, the Budweiser Rocket
3. Idaho's Snake River Canyon. Knievel failed when the parachute on his bike opened prematurely and sent him floating to the canyon floor.
4. The Miami Dolphins
5. Boris Spassky of the U.S.S.R.
6. Ilie Nastase
7. Probably not much, but it was the number of lengths by which he won the Belmont in 1973, thus making him the first horse in a quarter of a century to win the Triple Crown.
8. Mark "The Bird" Fidrych
9. Ping-Pong
10. Charlie Bauman
11. One of the seven teams that composed the first women's professional football league, founded in 1974
12. Darryl Dawkins of the Philadelphia 76ers
13. Frank Robinson; the Cleveland Indians
14. Pele
15. The New York Nets defeated the Denver Nuggets.

Movies 1

1. Howard Beale (Peter Finch), in *Network*
2. 2001 Oddyssey
3. Sensurround, which was supposed to let viewers experience a tremor by using loudspeakers to "shake" the theater, was introduced in *Earthquake*.
4. He/she ate a dog turd.

5. A KGB plot to destroy key U.S. military targets, in *Telefon*
6. During the football game, to keep time
7. The *Millennium Falcon*
8. *Valentino*
9. 956 years or life, whichever came first
10. *Mame*
11. Harry's cat
12. She was her reincarnated self
13. 28 hours; 400 cases of Coors
14. Callahan
15. Jimmy "Popeye" Doyle of *The French Connection*. (Unfortunately, Egan, who played Doyle's boss Simonson in the film, made only $240 from his part, and the New York City Police Department, unhappy with the film's portrayal of the department, fired Egan just 7 hours before he was due to retire on a full pension.)

TV Kids

Bradys
Bobby
Cindy
Greg
Jan
Marcia
Peter

Partridges
Christopher
Danny
Keith
Laurie
Tracy

Waltons
Ben
Elizabeth
Erin
Jason
Jim-Bob
John Boy
Mary Ellen

Bradfords
David
Elizabeth
Joannie
Mary
Nancy
Nicholas
Susan
Tommy

Richard Nixon

1. *Patton*
2. One thousand would be correct; he paid $878.03. (In March 1974, the IRS ordered Nixon to pay $432,787 in back taxes and interest for the years 1969–72.)
3. New York, where he had been disbarred that year
4. It was Nixon's name for the "Western White House" in San Clemente, California.
5. David Eisenhower
6. Ed Cox
7. Along with King Timahoe and Pasha, she was one of Nixon's three White House dogs.
8. Ketchup
9. Jimmy Hoffa's
10. He talked to it.
11. Prayed. Nixon's prayers weren't answered, but the nation's were.
12. Midair between Washington, D.C., and California
13. Secretary of State Kissinger
14. Hyden, Kentucky
15. The repeal of the 22nd Amendment, limiting presidents to two terms; and then, of course, a third term

First Lines 1

1. g
2. m
3. l
4. n
5. j
6. b
7. i
8. a
9. h
10. k
11. c
12. f
13. o
14. d
15. e

TV 2

1. Dan Shay
2. Archie Bunker, on *All in the Family*
3. Tina Louise
4. The *Little House on the Prairie*
5. These were the real names of Thaddeus Jones and Joshua Smith, on *Alias Smith and Jones*.
6. *Rhoda*, *Phyllis*, and *Lou Grant*

7. He was an eight-year-old evangelist who died when a TV fell into his bathtub and electrocuted him, on *Mary Hartman, Mary Hartman.*
8. The *Hawaii Five-O* team
9. *Funny Face* and *The Sandy Duncan Show*, played both times by Sandy Duncan
10. Reverend LeRoy, on *The Flip Wilson Show*
11. He was an architect, on *The Brady Bunch.*
12. George Carlin
13. The *Pacific Princess*
14. The *$1.98 Beauty Show*
15. The nurses on *Marcus Welby, M.D.*

News 2

1. Senator William Proxmire, D–Wisconsin
2. The Dalkon Shield IUD, produced by A. H. Robbins
3. It was the argument put forward by the attorney for former San Francisco Supervisor Dan White, whose assassination of Mayor George Moscone and Supervisor Harvey Milk in 1978 was ascribed to depression compounded by overconsumption of Twinkies and other junk food. In 1979 a jury returned a verdict of involuntary manslaughter due to "diminished capacity."
4. The profits made by oil-exporting countries, at the expense of Western nations, resulting from the dramatic increase in the price of oil during the preceding two years
5. The Reverend Sun Myung Moon
6. $2 million in free food
7. Sara Jane Moore and Manson groupie Lynette "Squeaky" Fromme
8. New York's La Guardia
9. No one; none was awarded
10. "Banana," as in "double-digit banana"
11. The MX, which stood for "missile experimental"
12. The neutron bomb
13. Four outside investigators were murdered by henchmen of the Reverend Jim Jones at the Guyana airstrip just before mass suicides began at Jonestown.
14. Allan Bakke; yes
15. Okinawa, which had been seized during World War II

20 Songs You're Going to Hate Us for Reminding You Of

1. p
2. i
3. l
4. e
5. a
6. b
7. d
8. g
9. c
10. q
11. m
12. n
13. f
14. r
15. s
16. k
17. j
18. h
19. o
20. t

Movies 2

1. The line was "No!" and it was spoken by Marcel Marceau.
2. Because, as he explained, he did "every dirty job that comes along"
3. Bunnies
4. The Cheyenne
5. Apollo Creed, played by Carl Weathers (it was the former pro football player's acting debut)
6. Dantooine; moon no. 4 of Yavin
7. John Lennon and Yoko Ono
8. Daisy; she was an Armenian sheep
9. Delta Tau Chi, in *National Lampoon's Animal House*
10. *Carnal Knowledge* (the U.S. Supreme Court later struck down the ruling)
11. *Family Plot*, in 1976
12. Vic Tayback
13. He shot her dog.
14. The spirits of dead Roman and Carthaginian generals
15. Danny Dravot (Sean Connery), in *The Man Who Would Be King*

Quotes 2

1. b
2. d
3. c
4. a
5. a
6. d
7. b
8. c
9. c
10. a
11. d
12. a
13. b
14. b
15. b

Boogie Fever

1. Percy Faith's
2. "Love to Love You Baby"
3. Indian chief, construction worker, cowboy, soldier, leather aficionado, and policeman
4. James Brown
5. "Disco Duck," by Rick Dees and His Cast of Idiots
6. A Quaalude
7. "Get Dancin'"
8. "I Love the Night Life"
9. "How Deep Is Your Love?" "You Should Be Dancing," "Jive Talkin'," "Stayin' Alive," "Night Fever," "Too Much Heaven," and "Tragedy"
10. *I Love Lucy;* the song was "Disco Lucy"
11. Pink Lady
12. Studio 54
13. "The Hustle"
14. "We Are Family"
15. John Travolta's co-star and disco partner in *Saturday Night Fever*

Watergate Whodunit

1. z
2. m
3. e
4. l
5. i
6. c, j, k, v or x
7. c, j, k, v or x
8. c, j, k, v or x
9. c, j, k, v or x
10. c, j, k, v or x
11. g
12. q
13. w
14. r
15. p
16. h
17. s
18. b
19. y
20. n
21. o
22. f
23. d
24. a
25. u
26. t

Trends

1. Burt Reynolds
2. Because the public mistakenly thought they contained red dye #2, which was banned in 1976 as a posssible carcinogen. They didn't.
3. Alaska's
4. Erhard Seminars Training. He was an encyclopedia salesman.
5. Cigarette advertising
6. First Lady Betty Ford
7. The Volkswagen Bug
8. Contraceptives
9. It was the first storm that the National Weather Service named for a man.
10. "Doonesbury"
11. He argued the legal concept of "palimony" for Michelle Triola Marvin, who had lived with but not married actor Lee Marvin. A Los Angeles judge denied her claim to half of Marvin's earnings for the years they had lived together, but did award her $104,000 to help her get a new start.
12. The hairstyle popularized in the mid-'70s by Olympic figure-skating champion Dorothy Hamill
13. Onions, rope, and toothpaste

14. Their daughter, Louise Joy, was the first "test tube" baby.
15. B. Kliban

Numbers—Relationships

1. e
2. b
3. a
4. j
5. d
6. c
7. h
8. i
9. f
10. g

People 2

1. For libel. During an unannounced tour of a Lexington franchise with a pack of reporters, Sanders had declared the food to be terrible. "My God, that gravy is horrible!" he'd exclaimed at one point. The Kentucky Supreme Court dismissed the company's suit against him.
2. He was Patty Hearst's live-in lover at the time of her kidnapping.
3. G. Harrold Carswell (who, incidentally, didn't get the job)
4. Muhammad Ali
5. Guru Maharaj Ji
6. Christo Javacheff
7. Pele
8. Mamie Eisenhower
9. He was upset that the San Francisco Giants had just lost a televised baseball game to the Houston Astros. "Didn't you ever want to shoot your TV?" he'd asked the arresting officers.
10. est founder Werner Erhard
11. Gregg Allman of the Allman Brothers Band. The marriage lasted 10 days.
12. From a toy whistle once found in Cap'n Crunch cereal. Phone phreaks found that this whistle had a 2,600-cycle tone that opened the Bell long-distance phone circuits. Draper, who before capture had traveled around the country in a VW bus with a computer and switchboard in the back, had once said, "It's possible for three phone phreaks to saturate the phone system of the nation. Busy it out. All of it."
13. Phyllis Schlafly

14. Isabel Perón of Argentina. (She didn't stay in power very long, despite the apparent connections of her advisers.)
15. Andrew Young

Disaster Movies

1. n
2. f
3. i
4. c
5. d
6. l
7. b
8. m
9. j
10. h
11. o
12. a
13. g
14. e (the fake)
15. k

Presidents for Life

1. Watergate
2. Lake Idi Amin Dada and Lake Mobutu Sese Seko, of course
3. His wife, Kay. (At least he didn't put her head in his freezer, which is where the noggins of some of his more illustrious opponents wound up.)
4. The $100-million affair was thrown by the Shah of Iran in the ruins of Persepolis to celebrate the 2,500th anniversary of the founding of the Persian Empire, which was destined to last 2,509 years altogether. Per capita income was $350 a year in Iran at the time, thus further endearing the Shah to his subjects.
5. The Chilean government of General Augusto Pinochet, which came to power in a 1973 coup. Because of death threats, the ad agency canceled its contract with Pinochet after one month.
6. Anastasio Somoza Bebayle, president of Nicaragua
7. Spanish dictator Francisco Franco, who died in 1975

8. Ferdinand and Imelda Marcos of the Philippines
9. Jean-Bedel Bokassa
10. Equatorial Guinea, ruled by Francisco Macias Nguema, who exiled a quarter of the population, killed all the intellectuals, and forced people into slavery
11. *The Dogs of War*
12. Kim Il Sung of North Korea. The communist diplomats proved inept at smuggling, and the plan quickly fell apart.
13. That of Francois "Papa Doc" Duvalier, his father
14. Egypt, Morocco, the Bahamas, Mexico, the U.S. (for medical treatment), and Panama
15. Pol Pot of the Khmer Rouge; Cambodia; Democratic Kampuchea

TV 3

1. Tiger
2. We were never told.
3. *Blood on the Badge*
4. Gerald Ford, who appeared on videotaped segments when his press secretary Ron Nessen was host
5. Major Margaret "Hot Lips" Houlihan, on *M*A*S*H*
6. Walt Whitman High School
7. *Carter County*
8. A red 1974 Ford Torino
9. Ernesta and Gwen Snoop wrote mysteries—although they weren't above occasionally dabbling in crime solving.
10. They worked on the assembly line in the bottle-cap division of Shotz Brewery in Milwaukee, on *Laverne & Shirley*.
11. Master Po and Master Kan
12. *Hawaii Five-O*
13. Boots the dog
14. He was the human-vegetable (or was that vegetable-human?) on *Quark*.
15. *The Los Angeles Tribune*

Songs 2

1. "You're So Vain" by Carly Simon
2. "Joy to the World" by Three Dog Night
3. "California" by Joni Mitchell
4. "Mamas Don't Let Your Babies Grow Up to Be Cowboys" by Waylon Jennings and Willie Nelson
5. "Sweet Baby James" by James Taylor
6. "Gypsies, Tramps and Thieves" by Cher
7. "If" by Bread
8. "We Are the Champions" by Queen
9. "Don't Bring Me Down" by the Electric Light Orchestra
10. "After the Gold Rush" by Neil Young
11. "Witchy Woman" by the Eagles
12. "Anarchy in the U.K." by the Sex Pistols
13. "Everything Is Beautiful" by Ray Stevens
14. "The Candy Man" by Sammy Davis, Jr.
15. "Our House" by Crosby, Stills, Nash & Young

Movies 3

1. His first film, in which he was dubbed, was *Hercules in New York*. He was billed as Arnold Strong.
2. The ship's cat
3. *The Song of Norway*
4. *Star Wars*
5. Three
6. *The Front*
7. "Steve!" (which was her boyfriend's name; he apparently had a memorable member)
8. The Replacement Party
9. *Jennifer* on *My Mind*
10. Dwan was a Libra, and she thought that Kong was an Aries.
11. The Pittsburgh Pisces
12. Devil's Tower, Wyoming
13. *Dementia 13*, which was co-producer Francis Ford Coppola's first directorial effort under his own name
14. It meant that a con was on.
15. Ray Milland and Rosie Grier

World News

1. Entebbe. Uganda's President Idi Amin was so angered by the raid that he ordered the execution of air traffic controllers and other personnel.
2. Nicosia, Cyprus
3. Steven Biko
4. Aldo Moro
5. Peking
6. The almost perfectly preserved body of his first wife, Eva. Anti-Perón governments had kept the body stashed in a secret location for years, but a pro-Perón faction had recently come to power and used the gift to entice the aging dictator to return to Argentina.
7. Lord Louis Mountbatten
8. The Orient Express between Paris and Istanbul
9. b
10. An unauthorized modern art exhibit in a field near Moscow
11. King Faisal
12. Salvador Allende Gossens, president of Chile, who was overthrown in a 1973 coup, also reportedly with CIA involvement
13. The Tasaday
14. It was the organization fighting to liberate Zimbabwe, then known as Rhodesia, from white minority rule.
15. The invasion of East Timor, a former Portuguese colony, by Indonesia

Real Shows? 1

1. *The Secret Empire*
2. *Curse of Dracula*
3. *Apple Pie*
4. *The Young Rebels*
5. fake
6. *Lucan*
7. *Turnabout*
8. *Time Express*
9. *Hizzonner*
10. *Fantastic Journey*

Women 2

1. They were among 53 prominent women who signed the American Women's Petition, asserting that they had had abortions, then illegal. The petition was published in a 1972 issue of *Ms.*
2. Probably three, although since Idaho, Nebraska, and Tennessee had rescinded their earlier approval—which no one seemed sure was legal—it may have been as many as six
3. Argentina. Vice President Isabel Perón became president on July 1, 1974, after her husband, President Juan Perón, died.
4. Gloria Steinem
5. They found Edelin guilty of manslaughter because, in their judgment, the fetus was already "viable." In 1977 the Massachusetts Supreme Judicial Court overturned his conviction.
6. She was fired, although a federal district court ruled that she could sue her employer for sex discrimination since male employees had not been required to wear such outfits.
7. Susan B. Anthony, a leader in the fight for women's voting rights. People rebelled against using the Susan B. Anthony dollar coin, complaining that because of its size it was too easily confused with a quarter.
8. Only one, William Rehnquist. Nixon's other three appointees (Warren Burger, Harry Blackmun, and Lewis Powell) voted in favor of it.
9. They retracted her title because she had said that being a beauty queen was not "a bed of roses."
10. The U.S. Marine Corps
11. Bella Abzug. Although the administration claimed that Abzug was fired for canceling a meeting and putting out a press release criticizing social spending cuts in Carter's new budget, Abzug, who was responsible for neither the meeting cancellation nor the press release, maintained that she was fired "because the President could not accept the criticism of his economic policies."
12. They were *all* anti-feminist organizations during the '70s.
13. It was the first college to have formal charges of sex discrimination filed against it.
14. The convict, who was incarcerated at the Iowa State Penitentiary (Fort Madi-

son) where Wyatt worked, charged that her presence "inflames the passions of prisoners." A federal district judge dismissed the suit.

15. The first battered women's shelter

Watergate Quotes

1. "stonewall"—Nixon
2. "toothpaste"—Haldeman, White House chief of staff
3. "inoperative"—Ziegler, Nixon's press secretary
4. "cancer"—Dean, White House counsel
5. "wallow"—Nixon
6. "twist . . . wind"—Ehrlichman, White House domestic affairs adviser, in reference to L. Patrick Gray's confirmation as director of the FBI
7. "third-rate"—Ziegler
8. "know . . . know"—Baker, member of the Senate Watergate Committee
9. "grandmother"—Colson, White House special counsel
10. "nightmare"—Ford, upon being sworn in as president

TV 4

1. Max the bionic dog, of course, on *The Bionic Woman*
2. On December 13, 1975, when NBC, fearing that host Richard Pryor might use obscene words, placed the show on five-second electronic delay
3. *Kate Columbo, Kate the Detective,* and *Kate Loves a Mystery* (her last name in this final series was Callahan)
4. An ex-Red Chinese agent, he was the primary enemy of Steve McGarrett and the rest of the Five-O team, on *Hawaii Five-O.*
5. Billy Carter
6. He once said, "I won't kill for it, and I won't marry for it. Other than that, I'm open to just about anything."
7. Ted Baxter, on *The Mary Tyler Moore Show*
8. *The Tim Conway Comedy Hour*
9. Oscar Madison, on *The Odd Couple;* he was a sportswriter
10. ESP
11. *Soap*
12. Ellery Queen, on *Ellery Queen*
13. Maya Angelou

14. They were the two actors who played Lionel Jefferson on *The Jeffersons* (and were not related).
15. He was the chief of staff at *Medical Center.*

Books 1

1. *Humboldt's Gift* by Saul Bellow
2. Also known as don Juan, he was the Yaqui Indian and sorcerer who taught author/anthropologist Carlos Castaneda to perceive "a separate reality," and whose teachings Castaneda described in a series of books.
3. In his 1978 book *In His Image: The Cloning of a Man*, Rorvik claimed that an elderly millionaire had been cloned, and that he had seen the 14-month-old cloned baby. He offered no proof, however, and scientists were skeptical that human cloning was possible using the techniques then available.
4. *The American Heritage Dictionary*
5. The Brooklyn Dodgers of the 1950s
6. *RN: The Memoirs of Richard Nixon*
7. M

8. Alex Haley; *Roots*. Haley reportedly paid Courlander $500,000 in an out-of-court settlement.
9. Although nine people were credited with the authorship, the book was actually written by a UNIVAC 1108 computer. The nine credited authors were the programmers at the University of Wisconsin who created the Novel Writer Simulation Program.
10. Agee was a disillusioned former CIA agent whose book, *Inside the Company*, was a behind-the-scenes story of the agency that also named names. The CIA, needless to say, was not overly pleased by this.
11. *The Late Great Planet Earth* by Hal Lindsay
12. Isaac Asimov
13. In the book, the police that the donkey parents went to for help were pictured as pigs.
14. Philip Roth, in his book *Our Gang*
15. Onassis was unhappy that Viking planned to publish *Shall We Tell the President?* a novel in which Edward Kennedy is president of the United States and the target of an assassination plot.

Who Did What? 1

1. i
2. e
3. d
4. c
5. a
6. b
7. l
8. j
9. f
10. n
11. h
12. k
13. o
14. m
15. g

Politics

1. Senator Richard Schweiker of Pennsylvania
2. Senator Robert Dole of Kansas
3. George McGovern
4. Nelson Rockefeller
5. John Connally
6. Senator Thomas Eagleton, whose failure to inform McGovern of his psychiatric record led to his removal from the ticket
7. R. Sargent Shriver, who replaced Eagleton on the ticket after five others turned McGovern down
8. Eagleton, of course, along with senators Hubert Humphrey, Edward Kennedy, Edmund Muskie, and Abraham Ribicoff, and Governor Reubin Askew
9. California Governor Jerry Brown, in 1979
10. George McGovern; President Nixon; Jimmy Carter
11. Representative Morris Udall of Arizona
12. He was angry with the right-wing Manchester *Union-Leader* for various personal attacks, including saying that his wife looked like a moll.
13. A small amplifier had blown and caused the loss of the audio portion of the program, and they were waiting for it to be repaired.
14. Dr. Benjamin Spock
15. The Democratic National Convention

Numbers—Disasters

1. d
2. g or h
3. f
4. c
5. b
6. i
7. a
8. e
9. j
10. g or h

Movies 4

1. *Fritz the Cat*
2. Navin Johnson (Steve Martin), in *The Jerk*
3. *High Anxiety*
4. *Play Misty for Me*
5. *Slapshot*
6. Zaza
7. *Interiors*
8. Maurice Ravel's "Bolero"
9. *Julia*
10. Lee Patrick and Elisha Cook, Jr.
11. Mildred, played by Joanne Woodward
12. *Pat Garrett and Billy the Kid*

13. Presbyterian Church
14. Paul Kersey
15. Ventana Nuclear Power Plant

People 3

1. Guru Maharaj Ji
2. Spiro Agnew. Despite whatever legal problems he may have had, he had no discernible connection to Watergate.
3. Tania
4. Malcolm Forbes
5. The famous Kent State shooting photo. Vecchio, a 14-year-old runaway, was the girl seen kneeling over the body of a fallen Kent State student.
6. She didn't take the obligatory stands: She admitted that she had smoked marijuana and refused to say that she was against premarital sex and abortion.
7. Yoko Ono
8. Werner Erhard, before he changed his name and founded est
9. He crashed his car through a White House gate. After stationing himself near the mansion, he managed to hold off police for four hours before finally

surrendering. They thought he had explosives, but what he really had were emergency warning flares.

10. She was the only passenger not rescued by the Israelis during their raid on Entebbe. Bloch had been taken to a Kampala hospital and was reportedly killed on orders of Idi Amin in reprisal for the raid.
11. Mother Teresa
12. Moore, who had appeared in public and on television as the Lone Ranger, could no longer wear his distinctive black mask. The company that owned the rights to the Lone Ranger planned to film a new Lone Ranger movie and didn't want an older Moore associated with the character. After the ruling, Moore took to wearing sunglasses instead.
13. Rosalynn Carter
14. Millicent Fenwick, R–New Jersey
15. Bill Cosby's. He received his Ph.D. from the University of Massachusetts in 1977.

True or False? 2

Items 7 and 9 are false (only Americans have walked on the moon, as far as we know anyway).

Music 2

1. The Sex Pistols
2. Elvis Costello
3. "Mama Told Me (Not to Come)," 1970; "Joy to the World," 1970; "Just an Old Fashioned Love Song," 1971; "Shambala," 1973; and "The Show Must Go On," 1974
4. Dawn, of Tony Orlando and Dawn
5. "Okie from Muskogee"
6. President Nixon
7. Newport officials were upset that more and more rock fans, looking for some kind of music festival to attend, were showing up in their fair city; they didn't want the jazz festival to become another Woodstock.
8. Carolyn
9. *Saturday Night Fever* by the Bee Gees, which sold 25 million copies
10. "Do Ya Think I'm Sexy?"

11. She hinted strongly that it was Warren Beatty. (Mick Jagger did the backup vocals.)
12. The Grateful Dead, in 1978
13. Haile Selassie's. As a Rastafarian, Marley believed that the Ethiopian emperor was divine.
14. Linda Ronstadt
15. Neil Diamond's

TV 5

1. The Brady kids, on *The Brady Bunch*
2. Chuckles, the clown on WJM's kiddie program, was trampled to death while dressed as a peanut by an elephant who was trying to shell him, on *The Mary Tyler Moore Show.*
3. *Swiss Family Robinson*
4. Mr. Bill, the very unlucky clay man on *Saturday Night Live,* had a dog named Spot.
5. *The Helen Reddy Show*
6. $200 a day, plus expenses
7. LeVar Burton and John Amos
8. Yeoman-Purser Burl Smith
9. *Barefoot in the Park*
10. *McMillan and Wife, Rhoda, The Nancy Walker Show,* and *Blansky's Beauties.* (While Walker also frequently appeared on the '70s episodes of *Family Affair* and on *The Mary Tyler Moore Show,* she was not a regular on those programs.)
11. The title was changed to *James at 16.*
12. She was killed in a plane crash, and *McMillan and Wife* became just plain *McMillan.*
13. They were the enemies of the people on *Battlestar Galactica.*
14. He owned a chain of dry-cleaning stores.
15. Captain Barney Miller, Detective Phil Fish, Detective Sergeant Chano Amenguale, Detective Stanley Wojohowicz, Detective Nick Yemana, Detective Ron Harris, and Detective Janice Wentworth (she only appeared during that first season)

Most Valuable Players

1. Robinson; Baltimore Orioles
2. Clemente; Pittsburgh Pirates
3. Tenace; Oakland A's
4. Jackson; Oakland A's
5. Fingers; Oakland A's
6. Rose; Cincinnati Reds
7. Bench; Cincinnati Reds
8. Jackson; New York Yankees
9. Dent; New York Yankees
10. Stargell; Pittsburgh Pirates

News 3

1. "Home on the Range"
2. Lockheed. In 1976 Japan's prime minister was forced to step down because of the scandal.
3. Fanne Foxe, whose real name was Annabella Battistella; Representative Wilbur Mills, D–Arkansas, chairman of the House Ways and Means Committee. Foxe leapt from Mills' car into the Tidal Basin after the vehicle was stopped by D.C. police.
4. Fifteen poorly dressed men who handcuffed the couple, ransacked their apartment, shouted obscenities, threatened their lives, and finally identified themselves as federal drug agents. The agents, who made their unannounced visit under the controversial "No Knock" law, had no search or arrest warrants, but they did have the wrong address. They were later indicted for their offenses.
5. A 4½-foot rattlesnake, planted there by members of the Synanon Foundation, who were angry that he had just won a $300,000 judgment against their cultlike drug rehabilitation organization. The snake, which attached itself to the attorney's left hand, was destroyed by the fire department, and Morantz was hospitalized and recovered from the bite.
6. Skokie, Illinois
7. Angela Davis
8. Frank Sinatra's
9. Massive busing to end racial segregation in schools
10. Juan Corona
11. Attendance by blacks; Jimmy Carter had always opposed the restriction

12. He was the Korean businessman charged, during the 1976 Koreagate scandal, with making questionable "contributions" to U.S. congressmen.
13. Several hundred Yippies were disrupting the Magic Kingdom by climbing buildings, staging their own circus, and singing the old Mickey Mouse Club song a bit too boisterously.
14. George Washington's
15. It was a collision, not a crash. The planes were on the fog-shrouded runway in Santa Cruz de Tenerife when the accident occurred, killing 582 people.

Enemies List

Muhammad Ali
Rona Barrett
Warren Beatty
Johnny Carson
Alistair Cooke
Bill Cosby
Henry Fonda
Peter Fonda
David Frye

Elliott Gould
Hubert Humphrey
Henry Jackson
Ethel Kennedy
Norman Lear
Rich Little
George Meany
Rob Reiner
Sargent Shriver
Tom Snyder
Gore Vidal

Movies 5

1. The words "Mafia" and "Cosa Nostra." (The League, incidentally, was headed by Anthony Columbo, the son of reputed mob boss Joe Columbo.)
2. Alderaan
3. He was a taxi driver, played by Robert De Niro, in *Taxi Driver*.
4. Drew (Ronny Cox)
5. *Sextette*
6. Vince Lombardi High
7. Billy Jack
8. The Bee Gees and Peter Frampton

9. Downed power lines on the wet ground angered the worms and brought them to the surface with a bad attitude.
10. *Harlan County, U.S.A.*
11. Sigerson Holmes, played by Gene Wilder
12. *Tess*
13. Jerry Lacy
14. They were the U.S. and U.S.S.R. orbiting missiles that were used to try to blast the meteor away from its collision course with Earth.
15. *You Light Up My Life*, of course

Gerald Ford

1. Lincoln
2. Whip Inflation Now
3. About eight pipefuls of tobacco daily
4. His middle name was Rudolph.
5. Iva Toguri D'Aquino, better known as Tokyo Rose
6. Visit Ford's Theater in Washington, D.C.
7. Eastern Europe. The comment, considered a major gaffe, was made during his second debate with Carter.
8. Except for Gerald Ford, it hated men.
9. Puerto Rico
10. Harry Truman's
11. Their yellow 1968 Buick LeSabre crashed into the presidential limousine after the Secret Service failed to have all the intersections on Ford's route blocked off.
12. The first lady said that she would want to know "if the young man were nice or not." Her failure to condemn the idea of an affair offended some conservatives, but a December 1975 *Time* poll showed that Americans overall agreed with her by a 64–23 percent margin.
13. George Bush
14. Golf balls. They set up a driving range in the hall.
15. *The Bees*

Events 1

1970 d
1971 g
1972 i
1973 h
1974 b
1975 c
1976 j
1977 e
1978 a
1979 f

Olympics

1. East Germany
2. To protest actions by officials that allowed the Soviet team to win in overtime. When the buzzer sounded at the end of the game, the U.S. had won, 50–49; but officials moved the clock back one second, and when the Soviets failed to score, back three seconds more. The Soviets finally scored and "won" the game.
3. Bruce Jenner
4. Seven; seven
5. Jim Naber
6. Rosi Mittermaier
7. Sapporo, Japan; Ard Schenk, who won his medals in speed skating
8. Seven cyclists from the Irish Republican Army crashed the event to prove that they were better athletes than the regular Irish contestants. One of them, however, definitely was not, and initiated the pileup.
9. Dorothy Hamill
10. Edwin Moses
11. For years he had used an asthma medication containing ephedrine, a stimulant forbidden at the Olympics. Although he had informed the U.S. Olympic Organizing Committee before the games, the U.S.O.C. had failed to discuss the subject with the appropriate officials and DeMont was forced to return the medal.
12. Sugar Ray Leonard, John Tate, and Leon and Michael Spinks
13. For cheating. Fencing is scored electronically, and his épée had been wired to register a hit even when he failed to touch his opponent.
14. Vassili Alexeev of the U.S.S.R.
15. Nadia Comaneci

Quotes 3

1. b
2. c
3. b
4. a
5. d
6. d
7. c
8. d
9. b
10. c
11. c
12. d
13. d
14. d
15. d

TV 6

1. *Shields and Yarnell*
2. Arthur Fonzarelli, on *Happy Days*
3. Paul Shaffer
4. The planet Ork, on *Mork & Mindy*
5. The show was *Charlie's Angels*, and she was billed as Cheryl Ladd.
6. Bob and Emily Hartley, on *The Bob Newhart Show*

7. She was a television production assistant at station KLXA in California. Her chief assignment was *The Paul Thurston Show*.
8. He was a yellow Labrador retriever police dog who patrolled L.A.'s streets with his partner, Officer Mike Breen.
9. Suzanne
10. Vinnie Barbarino, Juan Epstein, Freddie "Boom Boom" Washington, and Arnold Horshack, on *Welcome Back, Kotter*
11. A toothbrush
12. After John Amos quit the series, Rolle wanted producer Norman Lear to recast the role of the father to avoid the negative image of a black fatherless family. When he didn't, she quit the show.
13. Sam Fujiyama
14. The guest shots were intended to make children feel more secure by knowing that their two TV heroes were friends.
15. Bill Cosby, on the first *Bill Cosby Show*, which aired from September 1969 to August 1971

Endorsements

1. g
2. s or t
3. k
4. q
5. h or l
6. h or l
7. a
8. f
9. n
10. m
11. c
12. e
13. j
14. i or p
15. r
16. i or p
17. d
18. o
19. b
20. s or t

Women 3

1. Got her husband's signature
2. "Equality of rights under the law shall not be denied or abridged by the United States or by any State on account of sex."
3. Male chauvinism
4. The manager had been broadcasting a commercial for "chicks who can type," and they were obliging him.
5. It was a nationwide demonstration by women on August 26, 1970, the fiftieth anniversary of the Nineteenth Amendment, which gave women the right to vote. Participants demanded job and educational equality, more child care, and legalized abortion.
6. As a counterdemonstration to the Women's Strike for Equality, anti-feminists proposed that on September 30, 1970, every wife wear her frilliest dress, "sing before breakfast," serve her husband breakfast in bed, and "tell him how great he is."
7. They were, in 1978, the first women astronauts in the U.S. space program.
8. The magazine's female editorial staff revolted. *Newsweek*'s sole woman writer and 46 women researchers and

reporters filed a complaint with the Federal Equal Employment Opportunity Commission that they were "systematically discriminated against in both hiring and promotion and are forced to assume a subsidiary role simply because they are women." The women were particularly upset because the magazine had hired a freelancer to do the cover story.

9. A Texas state legislator, she came in second, after Tom Eagleton, in balloting for vice president at that year's Democratic convention and was the first woman whose name was placed in nomination for vice president at a major political party convention.

10. It eliminated sex-segregated classified ads, i.e., "Men Wanted" and "Women Wanted."

11. Soprano Beverly Sills had refused to sing unless Caldwell was allowed to conduct.

12. During the first season the only adult female human on the show was portrayed as a housewife. NOW felt that she should have a job, and the producers of *Sesame Street* agreed. The next season the character Susan had a job as a nurse.

13. Benazir Bhutto became prime minister of Pakistan and Margaret Thatcher became prime minister of Great Britain.

14. She was the first person to die as a result of the ban on Medicaid-funded abortions. Jiminez, who could not afford to pay for a doctor-assisted abortion herself, died at the hands of a cheap, illegal abortionist, leaving behind a five-year-old daughter.

15. She claimed self-defense, saying that he had tried to rape her. Except for his socks, the jailer was naked from the waist down when his body was found.

Numbers—Politics

1. d
2. i
3. a
4. j
5. e
6. c
7. f
8. h
9. b
10. g

Music 3

1. "I Think I Love You," "Doesn't Somebody Want to Be Wanted," and "I'll Meet You Halfway"
2. "Da Doo Ron Ron," which he sang on *The Hardy Boys Mysteries*
3. She was the girlfriend of Elvis Presley who discovered him dead on the bathroom floor on August 16, 1977.
4. Watkins Glen
5. Bob Dylan, who was booed by the audience
6. K.C. and the Sunshine Band
7. John Lennon
8. Ronnie Milsap (Charlie Pride was only named twice)
9. He was an Allman Brothers roadie found guilty in 1976 of distributing cocaine and other narcotics to Gregg Allman. Allman was granted immunity from prosecution in exchange for his testimony in the case.
10. Johnnie Taylor
11. Elton John
12. "The Captain" of the Captain and Tennille
13. Kinky Friedman and the Texas Jewboys
14. B. J. Thomas, Loretta Lynn, and Kenny Rogers and Dottie West
15. Herbert von Karajan of the Berlin Philharmonic

TV Expressions

1. Kojak
2. The Fonz
3. Chico Rodriguez
4. J. J. Evans
5. Geraldine
6. Florence ("Flo") Jean Castleberry
7. Steve McGarrett
8. Emily Litella
9. Tony Baretta
10. Sam McCloud
11. Mork
12. Fred Sanford
13. Archie Bunker
14. Any number of John Belushi characters
15. Roseanne Roseannadanna
16. The Fonz
17. Tattoo
18. Geraldine
19. Tony Baretta
20. Ted Baxter

Movies 6

1. The shark in *Jaws*
2. Ludwig van Beethoven
3. *Pumping Iron*
4. The dog was Blood. He was played by Tiger, who also starred in the TV series *The Brady Bunch* (proving himself a very versatile actor).
5. "Love" and "Hate"
6. Evelyn Draper (Jessica Walter)
7. *Shampoo*
8. They were dying from coronaries after having sex with the bee girls.
9. He played the hood who slit Jake Gittes' (Jack Nicholson's) nostril with a knife.
10. Desi Arnaz, Jr.
11. El Dorado, the fabled land of gold
12. *The Blue Bird*
13. *I Am Curious (Blue)*, of course
14. *Sleuth*
15. The Pharoahs

Trends 2

1. Packaged them as the Pet Rock, a product evidently so endearing that almost everyone got one that Christmas
2. The Cadillac Eldorado
3. Jacoby and Meyers
4. Abolitionist Harriet Tubman's
5. The Taser
6. Denim. The special edition 1973 Gremlin featured a denim landau roof and seats.
7. High-heeled shoes
8. Mia Farrow
9. Pies. Organizations with names such as Pie Face International and Pie-Kill Unlimited delivered the goods.
10. Homosexuality. The APA recommended passage of civil rights legislation to protect homosexual citizens.
11. COYOTE, based in San Francisco, was created to advance the rights of prostitutes.
12. After having several drinks, the California couple went into their 110-degree hot tub and passed out.
13. Ramtha, as channeled by J. Z. Knight
14. Doctors at the University of Minnesota Hospital gave him artificial blood, the first time it had been used in the U.S.

15. That black males be permitted to hold the priesthood

First Lines 2

1. e
2. i
3. m
4. a
5. j
6. d
7. l
8. c
9. o
10. f
11. b
12. k
13. g
14. n
15. h

Sports 2

1. New York Yankees owner George Steinbrenner
2. Reggie Jackson and George Steinbrenner
3. The first hot air balloon to make a transatlantic crossing, in 1978
4. To protest Muhammad Ali's return to boxing in a fight that night in Atlanta. Ali had offended right-wingers by refusing to be drafted three years earlier and had been shorn of his heavyweight title, but by 1970 the public's mood about the Vietnam War had changed enough, Maddox aside, for him to return to the ring. He defeated Jerry Quarry in his comeback outing.
5. Nancy Lopez
6. Ruffian. Efforts to save her were unsuccessful.
7. Coach Ted Marchibroda, who had been fired by Irsay after a disappointing exhibition season. The coach was rehired, and the team finished the season 11–3.
8. The Toronto Northmen, which later moved across the border and became the Memphis Southmen
9. The Cincinnati Reds

10. Joe Morgan
11. Affirmed; Steve Cauthen
12. The Iditarod
13. The Philadelphia 76ers, who lost 73 games in the '72–'73 season
14. Anatoli Karpov; Karpov won
15. Ted Turner

TV 7

1. The magic substance Feminum, which her belt and bracelets were made of
2. Maude Findlay, of *Maude*
3. The Bradys, on *The Brady Bunch*
4. *The Doris Day Show*
5. He was, arguably, psychologist Bob Hartley's most neurotic patient, on *The Bob Newhart Show.*
6. Theo
7. Gary Burghoff, who played Radar O'Reilly
8. The University of Wisconsin at Milwaukee
9. *My World and Welcome to It*
10. Jon Baker
11. Oscar's
12. She was Joe Mannix's secretary, on *Mannix.*

13. Barney Miller (no relation to the detective)
14. *Nichols.* It didn't help. By the time the twin made his appearance, the show had already been cancelled.
15. *Tomorrow*

Quotes—True or False?

Number 5 was never said.

Movies 7

1. The planet Transsexual
2. *The Lords of Flatbush*
3. John Shaft (Richard Roundtree), in *Shaft*
4. Depending on royalties, anywhere from $2.5 million on up
5. Canine HOMe Protection System
6. *Bugsy Malone*
7. *Dirty Harry*
8. *Murder by Death*
9. The cabaret in *Cabaret*
10. *Get to Know Your Rabbit*

11. *Swept Away . . . by an unusual destiny in the blue sea of August*
12. *Ode to Billy Joe*
13. *Harper Valley PTA*
14. Count Vladimir Dracula (George Hamilton), in *Love at First Bite*
15. *The Bad News Bears, The Bad News Bears in Breaking Training*, and *The Bad News Bears Go to Japan*

Which Came First?

1. Betamax (1975) was developed before VHS (1977).
2. The video game (1972) predated the shuttle (1977).
3. Heathcliff (1973) came before Garfield (1978).
4. Hoffa was gone (1975) before gambling came in (1978).
5. The first rabies vaccine was introduced in 1973; the Moral Majority was founded six years later.
6. *Look* ceased publication October 19, 1971; *Life* bit the big one December 29, 1972.
7. *Life* returned in 1978; *Look* returned in February 1979, died again August of that year, and has remained dead ever since.
8. The first instance of genetic engineering (1973) preceded the first female-to-male sex change (1977).
9. Miller Lite was introduced in 1975, one year before Perrier arrived.
10. Disney World (1971) preceded Jim Bakker's Heritage U.S.A. (1978).
11. In 1973 Sears Tower became the world's tallest building, superseding the World Trade Center, which had earned that honor in 1972.
12. MIT's Altair computer hit the marketplace in 1975, four years before the cube.
13. The CD was developed in 1970, nine years before Sony introduced its first Walkman.
14. Dr. Heimlich's lifesaving technique was first publicized in 1974, about two years before the Cuisinart showed up in stores.
15. The first black hole (Cygnus X-1) was located in 1971, two years before airlines began instituting baggage safety checks.

Music 4

1. Mick Jagger and Keith Richards
2. The Eagles
3. Little Richard
4. Grand Funk, which had, by their 1974 tour, dropped the "Railroad" from their name
5. Tina Turner
6. Donny, Marie, Alan, Wayne, Merrill, Jay, and Jimmy; "One Bad Apple," sung by most of the preceding
7. The Mahavishnu Orchestra
8. A dead skunk in the middle of the road. The song was called "Dead Skunk."
9. John and Christine McVie; Stevie Nicks and Lindsey Buckingham
10. Vicki Lawrence
11. Motown Records
12. Cincinnati; the Who
13. Zubin Mehta
14. Led Zeppelin
15. Bobby Sherman

Those Wonderful Nixon Years

1. The code name for the break-in at the Democratic National Headquarters in the Watergate office complex
2. Security guard Frank Wills, who received a $5-a-week raise as a reward
3. Nixon secretary Rose Mary Woods took credit for 4½ to 6 minutes of it. However, a panel of technical experts found that there were at least five separate erasures.
3. a. Chief
   b. Honor
   c. Massachusetts (the only state that voted for McGovern; he also won D.C.)
5. He was a former White House aide who was the first to reveal that White House conversations had been taped.
6. Martha Mitchell, wife of John Mitchell, former attorney general and head of CREEP
7. Dorothy Hunt, wife of E. Howard Hunt; her husband was one of the Watergate burglars
8. a. Elliot Richardson
   b. Archibald Cox
   c. William Ruckelshaus
   d. Robert Bork

9. a, b, c, and d are true; e and f are false—the Nixon forces preferred to run against McGovern, a weaker candidate than the others.
10. Donald Segretti, hired by White House aides with funds from CREEP

Blaxploitation Movies

The fake titles are *The Blaxorcist, Blackasaurus, Blackasaurus vs. Honkeytown, Afrodisiac Jones,* and *Pantherella.* (And the greatest sequel never made is *Blackasaurus Wrecks.*)

Journalism

1. Women were allowed to become members.
2. *Nightline,* in 1979
3. Hunter S. Thompson
4. For its dogged coverage of scandals and mayhem at the Synanon Foundation
5. *Rolling Stone*

6. A term used to describe Carl Woodward and Bob Bernstein, the two *Washington Post* reporters largely responsible for digging up the Watergate scandal
7. Well, there was an X-rated movie by that name starring Linda Lovelace . . . But more importantly, Deep Throat was the nickname given to a crucial source during Watergate by Woodward and Bernstein. Who it was, only they know.
8. Bolles was a reporter for *The Arizona Republic* investigating mob connections to Arizona racetracks. He died after a bomb planted in his car exploded. The last thing he said was "Adamson," the name of one of the figures he was investigating.
9. *Ms.*
10. *The Selling of the Pentagon,* about the Pentagon's self-promoting public relations activities. The full House voted not to cite CBS.
11. The Ayatollah Khomeini was not especially popular among American readers at the time.
12. Barbara Walters and Harry Reasoner; ABC
13. Walter Cronkite

14. Bill Stewart
15. To protest President Ford's pardon of Richard Nixon

Women 4

1. They could become Little League members. The Little League had made the change after being involved in numerous lawsuits that sought to open the program to girls.
2. Greta Rideout. In 1978 she accused him of raping her while they were living together, but he was ultimately acquitted by an Oregon circuit court.
3. It was a NOW-sponsored work stoppage by women on October 29, 1975, to show how much they contributed to the economy.
4. She was the first woman president of Planned Parenthood since Margaret Sanger, who had founded that organization in 1916.
5. Hawaii
6. One-half hour
7. The doll grew breasts when its arm was twisted. "We'll be happy when the development of a girl's mind receives as much attention as the development of her bosom," NOW declared.
8. Helen Reddy, accepting her award after winning "Best Pop, Rock, and Folk Vocal Performance—Female" for "I Am Woman"
9. Switzerland
10. It became the National Abortion Rights Action League and began work to ensure that abortions would remain legal.
11. Fourteen
12. Serve on juries. Lousiana automatically exempted women from jury duty until 1975, when the U.S. Supreme Court ruled that the exclusion of women was a violation of the Sixth Amendment, which provides that a defendant has the right to a jury drawn from a fair cross section of the community.
13. Ellen McCormack
14. Beverly Sills
15. Ella Grasso

Numbers—Sports

1. d
2. e
3. g
4. a
5. c
6. j
7. f
8. b
9. i
10. h

TV 8

1. Eve Plumb didn't return, and the role of Jan was played by Geri Reischl.
2. Orwell
3. Hawkeye Pierce, on *M*A*S*H*
4. To let her mother know she was all right
5. *Upstairs, Downstairs*, the British import that appeared on PBS's *Masterpiece Theatre*
6. Sue Ann Nivens, on *The Mary Tyler Moore Show*
7. Mrs. Livingston

8. *The Invisible Man* (of course) and *Gemini Man*
9. The Partridge Family's agent
10. She drank out of the "whites only" drinking fountain.
11. *Longstreet;* the dog was Pax
12. The two lead characters on *Adam 12*
13. The Osmonds, of *Donny and Marie*
14. Robert
15. David Letterman

People 4

1. Michelangelo's *Pietà*
2. Cheryl Tiegs. She later said that she didn't realize the suit was transparent.
3. Earl Butz
4. The Son of Sam was postal employee David Berkowitz, who terrorized New York City for more than a year with a string of six murders and seven attempted murders during 1976–77. Sam was a neighbor, Sam Carr. Berkowitz said that Carr's dog—and demons—told him to commit the murders.
5. Some said it stood for "Free the Army"; others had a different interpretation.

6. Albino Luciani
7. Thomas was charged with killing a Canada goose out of season after he clubbed the bird to death with a golf putter. He claimed that he had accidentally hit the goose with his approach shot and, discovering that it was wounded, had mercifully put it out of its misery with his golf club. Other golfers cried "fowl," however; they said that the goose had honked just as Thomas was about to take his shot and Thomas, upset at missing the shot, took his wrath out on the bird. The misdemeanor charges were dropped after Thomas paid a $500 fine.
8. Gerald Ford (he had taken his adoptive father's name) and Betty Ford (Betty was short for Elizabeth and Bloomer was her maiden name)
9. The services, 10 nights a month, of Judy Chavez, a prostitute with a specialty in sadism
10. Marshal Lon Nol of Cambodia
11. Princess Margaret, who divorced the Earl of Snowdon, Antony Armstrong-Jones, on May 24, 1978, after 18 years of marriage
12. Divine
13. Adultery
14. William O. Douglas. While the ostensible reason was Douglas's work for a foundation whose founder allegedly had gambling connections in Nevada, it was generally believed that the impeachment was desired because of Douglas's liberal leanings. A House committee found no evidence to support impeachment proceedings, however.
15. John Wooden

First Lines 3

1. d
2. j
3. g
4. i
5. m
6. c
7. e
8. l
9. n
10. b
11. h
12. o
13. f
14. a
15. k

Movies 8

1. At a funeral, in *Harold and Maude*
2. Organa
3. Matilda, in *Matilda*
4. "Puttin' on the Ritz"
5. It was the name of a movie and also the yacht featured in that film.
6. *Live and Let Die*
7. The two starring rats in *Willard*
8. *Myra Breckinridge*
9. The *Valley Forge*
10. George Segal and Jane Fonda, and they enjoyed robbing banks, in *Fun With Dick and Jane*
11. The North Dallas Bulls
12. He told her he was going on a business trip to Bakersfield.
13. *Big Bad Mama*
14. The Orca
15. Howard Cosell

TV Detectives

1. Peter Falk
2. Telly Savalas
3. William Conrad
4. James Garner
5. Raymond Burr
6. Buddy Ebsen
7. Robert Blake
8. Dennis Weaver
9. David Janssen
10. Rock Hudson
11. Burt Reynolds
12. Mike Connors
13. Jack Klugman
14. George Peppard
15. Richard Boone

Music 5

1. Peter Frampton, who "conversed" with the robot through a talk box that electronically distorted his voice through his guitar amplifier
2. "Ben," in 1972
3. The Talking Heads, in "Life During Wartime"

4. 1974
5. "Rapper's Delight"
6. The theme from *S.W.A.T.* by Rhythm Heritage and "Welcome Back" by John Sebastian, from *Welcome Back, Kotter*
7. Isaac Hayes
8. *Mass*
9. Loretta Lynn
10. Al Green
11. Jim Morrison
12. Elton John, on Thanksgiving 1974
13. Roger Daltrey
14. Jimmy Connors and Chris Evert
15. "Lady Marmalade" by Labelle

Goodbye, Vietnam

1. Nine
2. Jackson State
3. Buses
4. Ronald Reagan of California
5. The Pentagon Papers, a classified history of U.S. involvement in Vietnam
6. Besides unsuccessfully suing to keep the documents from being published, the White House "plumbers unit" burglarized the files of Ellsberg's psychia-

trist in an effort to find discrediting information.

7. Phony telegrams in support of the president's action

8. Nixon ended it; Carter restarted it.

9. To find out if they were using heroin; those who tested positive were put in detox programs. After two months of testing, 5.44 percent were found to have heroin in their bloodstreams from use within the previous 48 hours.

10. Because word leaked out that his chief of staff, H. R. Haldeman, was behind it.

11. Henry Kissinger and North Vietnamese politburo member Le Duc Tho, who together negotiated the Vietnam peace treaty in Paris

12. H. Ross Perot. The North Vietnamese ignored his offer.

13. Although he claimed he was only following orders, First Lieutenant William Calley, Jr., was sentenced to life in prison for the premeditated murder of 22 unarmed Vietnamese civilians in 1968. He was released from prison in 1974 by order of a civil court.

14. Bing Crosby's "White Christmas"

15. Ho Chi Minh City

True or False? 3

Items 5 and 8 are false (Castro was rooting for the Pittsburgh Pirates).

TV 9

1. *The Gong Show*

2. Radar O'Reilly's, on *M*A*S*H*

3. Taos, New Mexico

4. Taos, New Mexico. (No, we don't think they knew each other.)

5. Blanche Madison and Gloria Unger

6. Bing Crosby

7. The cop (played by George Kennedy) on *The Blue Knight*

8. J. I. Rodale. Cavett reported that while he was talking to his next guest, he looked over and saw Rodale "dozing" and asked, "Were we boring you, Mr. Rodale?"—then he realized that Rodale was dead. The show never aired. Rodale had said earlier during the June 7, 1971, taping, "I am so healthy that I expect to live on and on."

9. He had a solo program, *The Sonny Comedy Revue*, which only lasted

three months. Her solo program, *Cher*, lasted nearly a year but was never a great success. So, despite Cher's intervening marriage to Gregg Allman and birth of a son, the two of them joined up one more time to star in *The Sonny and Cher Show*. It was never as popular as its predecessor, though, and was canceled after two seasons.

10. Shirley
11. *Undercover Woman*, which was generally accepted to be a parody of real-life TV program *Police Woman*
12. The murder of his son. He wanted to track down his son's killer.
13. Chicken George
14. *Three's Company* and *Charlie's Angels*
15. He was the chimp on *Me and the Chimp*.

News 4

1. Billy Carter. While waiting for them to arrive in Atlanta, he was also seen urinating on the runway.
2. A toy pistol. Reagan, who had just announced his candidacy for the 1976 Republican nomination, was working a crowd at a Miami motel when the college dropout rushed toward him. Carvin was tackled by Secret Service agents and taken to a mental hospital.
3. Mikhail Baryshnikov, who had defected
4. *High Times*
5. Lettuce
6. Idi Amin
7. Hanafi Muslims. They feared *Mohammed, Messenger of God* would show an actor depicting the prophet, something they considered sacrilegious. Ironically, it didn't.
8. The *Queen Elizabeth I*, which was being renovated for use as a floating university
9. John Wayne Gacy of Norwood Park, Illinois, who killed 32 boys and buried most of them under his house and in his garage
10. Theodore Bundy, once a rising star in the Washington state GOP, was sentenced in 1979 for the murder of two young women attending college in Tallahassee, Florida. He was also suspected in dozens of similar crimes.
11. Native Americans, who had occupied the island for a year and a half and wanted to acquire title to it. Although 700 people had occupied the island at

one point, their number was down to 15 by the time the Feds arrived.

12. It was a Jesus festival attended by 80,000 young people at the Cotton Bowl in Dallas.
13. Hemorrhoids
14. The Gainesville Eight
15. Confucius

Quotes 4

1. a
2. d
3. c
4. d
5. b
6. d
7. d
8. a
9. d
10. c
11. a
12. b
13. a
14. a
15. b

People 5

1. Dummar, who ran a gas station in the desert, claimed that he had once given billionaire Howard Hughes a ride to Las Vegas and that, in turn, Hughes had left him a will naming Dummar as an heir. The will was not upheld in court.

2. The prize was actually awarded to Soviet dissident Andrei Sakharov, who was denied an exit visa to pick up the award, ostensibly because he could divulge military secrets. Sakharov's wife, Bonner, however, was already outside the country and could receive the award for her husband.

3. Part of his right ear, which was cut off in 1973 by kidnappers who wanted to show that they were serious in their ransom demands

4. Yes, 42 days. The original six counts he was charged with, which could have led to 50 years in prison, were plea-bargained down to one count of unlawful sexual intercourse. The judge wanted him to serve 90 days in prison, ostensibly for diagnostic testing. When the testing only took 42 days, however, the judge planned to send Polanski

back for an additional 48 days and also wanted Polanski, who was not an American citizen, to leave the country afterward. Rather than return to prison *and* have to leave the country, Polanski opted to just leave the country.

5. Olga Korbut's
6. Phyllis George
7. California Governor Jerry Brown, who acquired the nickname for his "spacey" views
8. Senator Harrison Schmitt (R–New Mexico), a former geologist and astronaut who had walked on the moon and was given the nickname by his colleagues in the Senate
9. Judy Chicago
10. Hall, a student skydiver, landed face down on an airport runway, but survived. "I screamed," he later recalled. "I knew I was dead and that . . . there was nothing I could do. It was all over." To his surprise, he suffered only a damaged nose and teeth, and got up and walked away. (He said that his life really did pass before his eyes.)
11. Princess Caroline of Monaco, on June 29, 1978
12. He objected to the speaker (liberal journalist I. F. Stone) and feared the possibility of student demonstrations.
13. It wasn't a man, and it was more than one. Twelve women—including Betty Ford, Barbara Jordan, Billie Jean King, and Susan Brownmiller—were chosen to represent not only themselves but also the "new consciousness" of all American women.
14. Pope John Paul II
15. Lucy was the name given to the fossilized remains of an early human found in Ethiopia in the fall of 1974. The skeleton, dated at 3 to 3.5 million years, was the most complete skeleton of that age ever found.

20 More Songs From Hell

1. Sammy Davis, Jr.
2. Marie Osmond
3. Paul Anka and Odia Coates. (No, she wasn't having his.)
4. Donna Fargo
5. America
6. Maria Muldaur
7. Mac Davis
8. Donny Osmond
9. Mary MacGregor
10. Freddy Fender
11. Wayne Newton
12. Maureen McGovern
13. Neil Sedaka
14. The Captain and Tennille; America
15. Ray Stevens
16. Eric Clapton
17. Gilbert O'Sullivan
18. Alan O'Day
19. Nilsson
20. Donna Fargo, again

Sports 3

1. Pittsburgh Steelers quarterback Terry Bradshaw threw a 73-yard pass to John Stallworth.
2. Washington, home of the city of Seattle
3. Lee Trevino
4. A rubber snake. Nicklaus laughed and went on to lose the tournament.
5. A mule. He named it Charlie O., of course.
6. She was the first woman signed to an NBA contract, in 1979. Meyers joined the Indiana Pacers but was cut after three days in training camp.
7. Racquetball
8. Giannoulas, who started his career as the San Diego Chicken in 1974, pretended to urinate on them.
9. Diana Nyad
10. Arthur Ashe
11. Due to a shortage of horsehide, they were, for the first time, covered with cowhide.
12. Dr. Renee Richards, known as Dr. Richard Raskind before her sex change operation. She ultimately had to go to court to prove that she was female, which she did.
13. Julius Erving; "The Doctor"

14. He was the NFL's first deaf player.
15. He won the first annual Empire State Building Run-Up, which involved 1,575 stairs and 86 floors.

Movies 9

1. "An omelet, plain, and a chicken salad sandwich on wheat toast—no mayonnaise, no butter, no lettuce—and a cup of coffee. . . . Now hold the chicken salad, bring me the toast, give me a check for the chicken salad sandwich, and you haven't broken any rules."
2. A "black capsule" (which wasn't really meant to kill him at all)
3. July 14. That was "French independence day" and the troops were expected to be drunk.
4. *Star Wars*. They played C-3PO and R2-D2.
5. *Deep Throat*
6. *Rabbit Test*
7. Nineteen curtain calls
8. *Goin' Coconuts*. They played Donny and Marie Osmond—not a hard stretch, even for them.

9. Vger, which had originally been a Voyager spacecraft a few centuries before
10. She wanted him to find her kidnapped cat.
11. Sissy Spacek. She did her own singing.
12. "I remember"
13. *Pretty Baby*
14. He was looking for water for his planet.
15. *Sweet Sweetback's Baadasssss Song*

Numbers—Women

1. d
2. c
3. g
4. i or j
5. a or b
6. f
7. e
8. i or j
9. h
10. a or b

Jimmy Carter

1. Confederate President Jefferson Davis
2.   a. 2
       b. 5
       c. 4
       d. 3
       e. 1
3. Billy, defeated 90–71, in his bid to become mayor of Plains, Georgia
4. Lust
5. Sexual desires. The freelance interpreter, hired for $150 per day by the State Department, also told the crowd that Carter had not merely left the U.S. that morning, he had abandoned it forever.
6. For disturbing the peace by playing her harmonica louder than the jukebox and refusing to leave
7. A drink. No hard liquor was served, although wine was served after dark.
8. a and c
9. Rabbit
10. *What's My Line*, and he almost stumped the panel
11. *The Best*. It was the title of Carter's '76 campaign book.
12. Out of respect for the American hostages in Iran
13. a, c, d, and e
14. Carter recounted for Mexican President Jose Lopez Portillo how he had gotten "Montezuma's Revenge" (a.k.a. diarrhea) on a previous visit.
15. She sat in on cabinet meetings

Who Did What? 2

1. h
2. e
3. k
4. g
5. j
6. a
7. m
8. f
9. l
10. n
11. b
12. c
13. i
14. o
15. d

TV 10

1. Dan Aykroyd, John Belushi, Chevy Chase, Jane Curtin, Garrett Morris, Laraine Newman, and Gilda Radner. (Bill Murray joined the show during the second season as a replacement for Chevy Chase, who had left to pursue a career in movies.)
2. The Dallas Cowboys Cheerleaders, in the movie of the same name
3. He was Alice Nelson's love interest on *The Brady Bunch*.
4. He was the San Francisco police commissioner. Sally McMillan's father had been a police commissioner as well.
5. The original *Rookies*
6. *Pat Paulsen's Half a Comedy Hour*
7. Owen Marshall, on *Owen Marshall, Counselor at Law*
8. Hers was the voice of the dispatcher on *Adam 12.*
9. *Beacon Hill.* It lasted only 13 episodes.
10. Redd Foxx, the actor who played the character. Foxx's real name was John Sanford.
11. Carlton, played by Lorenzo Music
12. The band on *Fernwood 2-Night*
13. *Makin' It*
14. They were the actors who played Christopher and Tracy Partridge on *The Partridge Family*.
15. Benjamin Franklin Pierce

The Oscars

1. *One Flew Over the Cuckoo's Nest*
2. Sacheen Littlefeather
3. Maria Cruz
4. Tatum O'Neal, who won the Best Supporting Actress award for *Paper Moon*
5. He streaked across the stage.
6. Lina Wertmuller, for *Seven Beauties*. She didn't win.
7. Vanessa Redgrave
8. Paddy Chayefsky
9. *The Godfather II*
10. Peter Finch, who won the Best Actor Oscar for *Network*
11. Eleven young girls, who were said to be affiliated with the John Tracy Clinic for the Deaf, provided a simultaneous translation of the song into American Sign Language.
12. Newspapers later revealed that the girls were actually students from Tor-

rance, California, and their "signing" was nonsense.

13. *Le Charme Discret de la Bourgeoisie (The Discreet Charm of the Bourgeoisie)*

14. Clint Eastwood. The audience roared as Eastwood read lines off the teleprompter that had been written for Heston, with jokes about Moses and *The Ten Commandments*. "This isn't my bag, man," he complained shortly before Heston finally showed up.

15. It was the first time she had ever attended the Academy Awards ceremony, having turned down her previous 41 invitations.

Songs 3

1. "Knock Three Times" by Dawn
2. "Happiest Girl in the Whole U.S.A." by Donna Fargo
3. "You're the One That I Want" by John Travolta and Olivia Newton-John
4. "Life's Been Good" by Joe Walsh
5. "Running on Empty" by Jackson Browne

6. "The Way We Were" by Barbra Streisand
7. "Head Games" by Foreigner
8. "Goodbye Yellow Brick Road" by Elton John
9. "Stayin' Alive" by the Bee Gees
10. "Take the Long Way Home" by Supertramp
11. "Cat's in the Cradle" by Harry Chapin
12. "Smoke on the Water" by Deep Purple
13. "Another Brick in the Wall (Part I)" by Pink Floyd
14. "Disco Lady" by Johnnie Taylor
15. "Summer Breeze" by Seals and Crofts

The Environment

1. They were celebrating the first Earth Day.
2. It was, in 1978, the first species removed from the endangered species list since the passage of the Endangered Species Act in 1973. It was removed because it was believed to be extinct.
3. Karen Silkwood, who worked for the Kerr-McGee Corporation in Cimarron, Oklahoma

4. Swordfish
5. Federal clean air standards
6. Kepone, used in insecticides
7. The Alaska pipeline
8. Because the fish were contaminated with PCBs, or polychlorinated biphenyls
9. Phosphates in detergents
10. The children had eaten meat and poultry that had been injected with estrogen.
11. Because the structure threatened the survival of the snail darter, a three-inch-long fish protected under the Endangered Species Act
12. The SST aircraft, which the U.S. decided against developing
13. Love Canal
14. Vinyl chloride, which along with its derivative, polyvinyl chloride, was used extensively in plastics manufacturing and as a propellant in aerosols
15. Brown's Ferry, in Alabama

Advertising

1. That it built strong bodies 12 ways; in 1973 an FTC administrative judge dropped the case
2. He said that its high phosphate content could contribute to pollution.
3. Joe Namath
4. Sony's "tummy television"
5. The Volkswagen Beetle
6. The Frito Bandito
7. Tramps
8. Euell Gibbons in Grape Nuts commercials
9. National
10. "We really move our tail for you"
11. Mikey, played by John Gilchrist
12. Barry Manilow
13. Orson Welles
14. Mason Reese
15. Marilyn Chambers

Real Shows? 2

1. *Struck by Lightning*
2. *The Immortal*
3. *Baby, I'm Back*
4. *A Year at the Top*
5. *The Good Life*
6. fake
7. *Out of the Blue*
8. *UFO*
9. *Holmes and Yoyo*
10. *Man From Atlantis*

People 6

1. Resurrect the frozen body of his mother
2. "Self-urine" therapy. Said Desai, "For the past five or six years I have drunk a glass of my own urine—about six to eight ounces—every morning. . . . Urine is the water of life."
3. They traded wives. While still married, Kekich's wife, Suzanne, went to live with Peterson, while Peterson's wife, Marilyn, went to live with Kekich. Eventually Kekich and Marilyn Peterson broke up, but Peterson and Suzanne Kekich remained together.
4. She collapsed after drinking gin and tonic, mixed with small doses of Librium and Valium, with friends.
5. Representative Wayne Hays, D–Ohio. She was his mistress.
6. Boris Spassky
7. He was a Nixon look-alike who made a career out of impersonating Nixon in films during the '70s.
8. Fegion said that her husband "chases girls."
9. During his voyage, Mitchell sent information telephathically to four people on Earth. He reported that his receivers got a statistically significant number of correct answers.
10. James Irwin
11. Spiro Agnew
12. The first all-male beauty pageant, in Boston. Le Clair was crowned Adonis '72.
13. He was the ski-ace lover of Claudine Longet, whom she accidentally shot to death in 1976 in Aspen. She was found guilty of criminally negligent manslaughter for the death and sentenced to 30 days in jail.
14. He had been caught writing improper prescriptions for Quaaludes.

15. Sun Myung Moon, of course, and it was approximately 1,800 couples who tied the knot in Seoul, South Korea, in 1975

Numbers—News

1. f
2. c
3. b
4. d
5. i
6. a
7. e
8. j
9. g
10. h

TV 11

1. It was the moon, which had been accidentally blasted free of its Earth orbit.
2. He was an informant for *Starsky and Hutch*.
3. *Love, American Style*
4. *Mary* (a comedy variety show that lasted only three broadcasts) and *The Mary Tyler Moore Hour* (a comedy variety-situation comedy that aired for three months)
5. Killer
6. Harry-O, on the show of the same name
7. Freddy Prinze, who played Chico, had committed suicide the previous season, and his absence was explained in this way.
8. He was the leader and prophet of an invisible cult, the Friends of Venus, on *Mork & Mindy*.
9. SCTV (channel 109), on *Second City TV*
10. Mike and Gloria Stivic's baby was called Joey.
11. The Bellamy family and their servants, in *Upstairs, Downstairs*
12. Banner turned into the Hulk whenever he became angry.
13. *It's a Wonderful Life*
14. Barney, on *Lou Grant*
15. James J. Kilpatrick was the conservative. Nicholas Von Hoffman was the liberal for the first year and Shana Alexander was the liberal for the rest of the feature's run.

Music 6

1. "My Way"
2. Frank Zappa
3. Karen and Richard Carpenter
4. Willie Nelson
5. The Sound of Philadelphia (music with a beat influential in the development of disco music); Mothers, Fathers, Sisters, Brothers
6. The Philadephia Orchestra; Tchaikovsky's "1812 Overture"
7. We were spared b and c.
8. "Rise"
9. He was an alter ego of David Bowie.
10. Robin Williams, of course
11. Olivia Newton-John of Australia was named Female Vocalist of the Year, leading more traditional performers to complain that the CMA was abandoning "authentic" country music.
12. "I Don't Like Mondays," which the teenager, Brenda Spencer, gave as her reason for the shooting
13. *The Rolling Thunder Revue*
14. The cover was changed when, five days after the album made its debut, three members of the band were killed in a fiery plane crash.
15. Alice Cooper. A public audition for a new snake was held, and a boa named Angel got the job.

First Lines 4

1. l
2. h
3. o
4. f
5. k
6. a
7. m
8. g
9. n
10. c
11. b
12. i
13. d
14. j
15. e

Movies 10

1. Howard Hawks' *Red River*
2. *Grease*
3. He was dead.
4. *The Sorrow and the Pity*
5. Her parents didn't give her shoes with cha-cha heels for Christmas.
6. Richard Wagner's "Ride of the Valkyries"
7. The Ecumenical Liberation Army
8. *A Party at Kitty and Stud's (The Italian Stallion)*
9. "That's OK, 'cause we don't eat 'em, neither."
10. *Airport 1975*
11. He was a dog and he saved Hollywood, in *Won Ton Ton, the Dog Who Saved Hollywood.*
12. Linda Blair's "vomit" in *The Exorcist*
13. John Houseman
14. *The Naked Ape* by Desmond Morris
15. Bertolucci showed actress Maria Schneider nude throughout much of the film, but did not include the nude scenes he'd shot of Marlon Brando.

Events 2

1970 h
1971 f
1972 d
1973 a
1974 i
1975 b
1976 g
1977 j
1978 c
1979 e

Theater

1. *Jesus Christ Superstar*
2. *Lemmings*
3. *For Colored Girls Who Have Considered Suicide/When the Rainbow is Enuf*
4. The cast of *Grease*
5. "Tomorrow, tomorrow, it must be tomorrow"—from *Annie*, in which she played the title role when it opened on Broadway in 1976
6. *Got Tu Go Disco*
7. Tom Stoppard

8. Eight
9. *The Wiz*
10. *When You Comin' Back, Red Ryder?*
11. *Lorelei*
12. *Pippin*
13. They were baked into pies.
14. *Two Gentlemen of Verona*
15. *Buck White*

Space

1. The rings of Uranus
2. Soyuz
3. On Io, the innermost of Jupiter's four largest moons
4. Apollo 17; Eugene Cernan
5. Charon. In Greek mythology, Charon was the boatman who ferried the souls of the dead across the River Styx to Hades, where Pluto sat in judgment.
6. c and d
7. Mariner 9; Mars
8. It didn't take place. An oxygen tank rupture midway to the moon caused the mission to be aborted, and the astronauts returned home after circling the moon (the easiest way back) in the lunar module.
9. Probably not. Puzzling chemical reactions, which at first had led some scientists to speculate that the spacecraft had discovered either a new form of life or a new form of chemistry, are now generally believed to be due to the nature of the Martian clay.
10. Like ringed Saturn and Uranus, Jupiter was also found to have a ring.
11. Salyut 1, in April 1971
12. Venus; Venera 9 and Venera 10
13. David Scott, Alfred Worden, and James Irwin (the crew of Apollo 15). They were reprimanded, and two of them were dropped from the astronaut corps and reassigned to other jobs in NASA; the third resigned.
14. When the abandoned space station Skylab reentered the earth's atmosphere on July 11, 1979, NASA officials delayed the descent to avoid hitting populated areas in North America, which caused some parts of Skylab to fall safely into the Indian Ocean—but many other pieces fell onto Australia. Small pieces hit rooftops in Perth, and one 1,870-pound, six-by-three-foot chunk shook the Australian countryside when it landed near Rawlinna. "I think it stinks that they delayed the de-

scent so it missed them and hit us," said one Perth woman. And the American consulate in Perth was deluged with phone calls protesting a remark by a NASA spokesman that the only risk was to "a wallaby or two." There were no reported injuries, however— not even to a wallaby.

15. Cosmos 954

Quotes 5

1. c
2. b
3. a
4. b
5. d
6. b
7. c
8. a
9. b
10. b
11. b
12. b
13. b
14. c
15. b

Books 2

1. Clifford Irving. He was sentenced to 2½ years in prison and fined $10,000. Publisher McGraw-Hill also won a $776,000 judgment against him.
2. Saul Bellow won in 1976, and Isaac Bashevis Singer, who, although not born in the U.S., was a naturalized citizen, won in 1978.
3. *Sleeping Murder*
4. *Islands in the Stream*
5. *The Silmarillion*
6. Xaviera Hollander
7. *Our Bodies, Ourselves* by the Boston Women's Health Book Collective, a self-help guidebook for women about their bodies, their health, and their sexuality
8. Ecotopia, a mythical land in Ernest Callenbach's book of the same name, comprised Washington, Oregon, and Northern California.
9. Although the Pulitzer fiction jury unanimously recommended Thomas Pynchon's *Gravity's Rainbow* for the award, they were turned down by the advisory board. Some members of the board reportedly found the book unreadable and, occasionally, obscene. Jury and board were so sharply di-

vided that they opted to give no award that year. (*Gravity's Rainbow* did win the National Book Award that year, however.)

10. Spiro Agnew
11. Muhammad, the prophet of Islam
12. *Baby and Child Care* by Dr. Benjamin Spock
13. *Breakfast of Champions* and *Jailbird*
14. *Elvis: What Happened?*
15. *Ball Four*

Numbers—Economics

1. d
2. j
3. e
4. a
5. h
6. c
7. b
8. i
9. g
10. f

Movies 11

1. Black
2. *The Trial of Billy Jack*
3. *Flesh Gordon*
4. By running down pedestrians
5. *Jonathan Livingston Seagull*
6. The Godfather, in the film of the same name
7. *Fists of Fury*, a.k.a. *The Big Boss*
8. *Mackintosh and T.J.*
9. *Two Minute Warning*
10. *THX 1138*
11. They were Willy Wonka's (Gene Wilder's) helpers, in *Willy Wonka and the Chocolate Factory*.
12. Ivy Templeton, in *Audrey Rose*
13. They were the vicious gang of cyclists in *Mad Max*.
14. *The Gospel Road*
15. It was the code name of the project to discover the cause and cure for the deadly virus in *The Andromeda Strain*.

Who Did What? 3

1. j
2. o
3. f
4. m
5. g
6. a
7. c
8. l
9. b
10. n
11. h
12. e
13. i
14. d
15. k

Trends 3

1. Crunchy Granola
2. Cheryl Tiegs
3. Jump ropes
4. Vegimels, introduced in time for Christmas 1977, were stuffed cloth toys resembling vegetables. Probably due to a lack of cuddly, anthropomorphic qualities, they never caught on.
5. *Rolling Stone*
6. *Primal Scream*
7. Howard Jarvis, a retired businessman and head of a Los Angeles landlord lobbying association, and Paul Gann, a retired real estate salesman and president of a taxpayers' association
8. est's
9. Nonparent's Day
10. Preparation H, the hemorrhoid medication. It irritated the skin and caused enough swelling to minimize small wrinkles, but doctors warned that its long-term use could lead to inflammation and scaling.
11. Skateboards
12. Worms (although spider eggs and kangaroo meat were also making the rounds at the time). At one point company officials were reduced to explaining that it didn't make economic sense to use worm meat because wholesale earthworms were much more expensive than beef.
13. Sports locker rooms, to which female reporters were admitted for the first time
14. Gay Bob
15. Condoms

Music 7

1. Funkadelic. The group's founder, George Clinton, was quoted as saying, "Funk is its own reward."
2. Wildfire
3. To raise money for war victims in Bangladesh, formerly East Pakistan, which had declared independence from Pakistan that year
4. Scott Joplin; *Treemonisha*
5. The Blues Brothers (a.k.a. Dan Aykroyd and John Belushi)
6. The Oak Ridge Boys
7. Ayatollah Khomeini of Iran
8. Kenny Rogers
9. They were charged with bribing radio station employees to plug their records.
10. Bette Midler; Barry Manilow
11. *The Harder They Come*
12. The Opry was about to be moved from the Ryman Auditorium to a new building on the outskirts of Nashville. Many performers felt that the move signaled the triumph of commercialism over grass-roots country, while others were not happy that the new location was in a "dry" county where no liquor was available.
13. Stevie Wonder
14. George Benson
15. "The Streak"

True or False? 4

Items 3 and 7 are false.

TV 12

1. Walter, on *M*A*S*H*
2. He was quitting smoking, and the lollipops served as a substitute for cigarettes.
3. Florida Evans, Mrs. Nell Naugatuck, and Victoria Butterfield
4. Tony's pet cockatoo was named Fred, on *Baretta*.
5. *Laugh-In*, the short-lived successor to *Rowan and Martin's Laugh-In*
6. On *The Muppet Show* (Captain Link Heartthrob was commander of the starship *Swinetrek*)
7. Carl Kolchak, of *Kolchak: The Night Stalker*
8. Dwayne

9. Bill Bixby, who was an amateur magician, performed his own tricks on the series.
10. Lawrence
11. Wolfman Jack
12. Monte Markham, on *The New Adventures of Perry Mason*
13. Kelsey's Bar. He renamed it Archie's Place, on *All in the Family* and *Archie Bunker's Place*.
14. *Monty Python's Flying Circus*
15. The Fonz

Stranger Than Fiction

1. d
2. f
3. e
4. g
5. b
6. c
7. h
8. i
9. j
10. a

Women 5

1. Sonia Johnson
2. The First National Women's Conference
3. She was the Jane Roe in *Roe* v. *Wade*
4. The chador, an all-enveloping veil that covers a woman from head to toe. The demonstrations worked; the government backed down, saying it had merely been suggesting modest dress.
5. Representative Martha Griffiths (D–Michigan)
6. They felt that her low salary (which she obviously didn't need anyway) was holding down women's wages.
7. Billie Jean King in 1972 and Chris Evert Lloyd in 1976
8. Rape. Simonson created a public outrage when he said that a 15-year-old boy who had raped a 16-year-old high school girl was reacting "normally" to provocative clothing and lax moral standards in the community. The judge then gave the rapist probation. Voters in the county disagreed with him, however, and held a recall election in which Simonson was defeated by the only woman in the six-person race.
9. Women's International Terrorist Conspiracy from Hell

10. Marabel Morgan in *The Total Woman*
11. They had to be sterilized. The company declared that women of reproductive capability would be barred from jobs with exposure to lead compounds.
12. Shirley Chisholm, in 1972
13. They were protesting their organization's endorsement of the ERA.
14. More women than men entered college.
15. They refused to hire her because she had preschool-age children. The U.S. Supreme Court, however, ruled in 1971 that Martin Marietta had violated the law unless they also refused employment to men with young children.

News 5

1. Frasier
2. Burt Reynolds (but they didn't put *him* out with the lionesses)
3. Carter was referring to the problems poor women would face because of restrictions, which he favored, on federal funding for abortions.
4. The People's Republic of China

5. Restrict smoking in public places
6. Ronald Reagan and Prince Charles
7. Paraquat
8. The Soviet Union. Competitors in this sport—dubbed "Ready for Work and the Defense of the U.S.S.R."—used deactivated grenades.
9. The biological clock
10. They started eating the 29 people who had died. The rescue occurred 69 days after the October 13 plane crash.
11. The House Committee said that it was "likely" that a conspiracy to kill Kennedy did exist and that there was a "high probability" that a second gunman fired at the president.
12. James Schlesinger. He was secretary of defense under Nixon and Ford and secretary of energy under Carter.
13. The craft, scientists determined, had suddenly depressurized due to a leak in its hatch system.
14. Arcosanti
15. Bon Vivant

Super Bowls

1. Chiefs–Vikings
2. Colts–Cowboys
3. Cowboys–Dolphins
4. Dolphins–Redskins
5. Dolphins–Vikings
6. Steelers–Vikings
7. Steelers–Cowboys
8. Raiders–Vikings
9. Cowboys–Broncos
10. Steelers–Cowboys

7. Bob Crane
8. Nixon, in 1974
9. Disco records
10. Jimmy Carter
11. *Over There*
12. Milligan, accused in the rapes of four Ohio State women, claimed that he had multiple personality disorder and that the rapes were committed by his lesbian personality.
13. Richard Nixon
14. Tugboat
15. Jimmy, Rosalynn, and Amy Carter

People 7

1. California Governor Jerry Brown
2. Economist E. F. Schumacher
3. Comedian Steve Martin
4. Grace Slick. When Slick arrived with antiwar radical Abbie Hoffman as an escort, he was denied admission, so she left with him. Slick also had threatened to spike Ms. Nixon's tea with LSD.
5. They were upset that Brennan, the court's only Catholic, had ruled in favor of *Roe* v. *Wade*.
6. D. B. Cooper

Movies 12

1. *The Shootist*
2. *Close Encounters of the Third Kind*
3. A box of Raisinets
4. *Godzilla vs. the Smog Monster*
5. *At Long Last Love*
6. *Snuff*
7. Clyde
8. What is your name? What is your quest? What is the capital of Assyria?
9. Greedo
10. Joe Namath

11. *Johnny Got His Gun*
12. Jack Crabb (Dustin Hoffman), in *Little Big Man*
13. *Alien* (he played the alien)
14. $2,000
15. *The Greek Tycoon*

Songs 4

1. "I Am . . . I Said" by Neil Diamond
2. "Midnight Train to Georgia" by Gladys Knight and the Pips
3. "Killing Me Softly With His Song" by Roberta Flack
4. "Yank Me, Crank Me" by Ted Nugent
5. "Brand New Key" by Melanie
6. "Fly Like an Eagle" by the Steve Miller Band
7. "I Think I Love You" by the Partridge Family
8. "Takin' Care of Business" by Bachman-Turner Overdrive
9. "Don't Stop" by Fleetwood Mac
10. "Piano Man" by Billy Joel
11. "I Write the Songs" by Barry Manilow
12. "Rhinestone Cowboy" by Glen Campbell

13. "Tie a Yellow Ribbon Round the Ole Oak Tree" by Tony Orlando and Dawn
14. "Smokin' in the Boys' Room" by Brownsville Station
15. "Ripple" by the Grateful Dead

TV—Killer Questions

1. The shows were *The Hudson Brothers Show*, *The Hudson Brothers Razzle Dazzle Show*, and *Bonkers*; the Hudson Brothers were Bill, Brett, and Mark.
2. *The Hanna-Barbera Happy Hour.* Honey and Sis were the puppets.
3. Their two English bulldogs, Elizabeth and Broderick
4. ABC's *Delta House* (this one was the closest to the movie and had four of the film's stars), CBS's *Co-Ed Fever* (this one was so bad that it only aired once), and NBC's *Brothers and Sisters*
5. The Eskimo friend of Officer Cal "Kodiak" McKay, on *Kodiak*
6. *Miss Winslow and Son*
7. The troublesome bear in Sierra National Park, on *Sierra*
8. *Roll Out*

9. Father Tony Curtis and daughter Jamie Lee Curtis were both in *Operation Petticoat*.
10. She was an 80-year-old grandmother and the winner of the "Anyone Can Host" write-in contest on *Saturday Night Live* (and, of course, host of the program).
11. *A Year at the Top*
12. John Keane was the 12-year-old and Tim was 13. The program was *The Keane Brothers Show.*
13. Diana Hyland, who had played Joan Bradford
14. *All That Glitters*
15. *Adams of Eagle Lake*

'70s Graduate Exam

1. Bjorn Ulvaeus, Benny Andersson, Agnetha Faltskog, and Anni-Frid "Frida" Lyngstad
2. Wang Hungwen, Chang Chungiao, Jiang Qiang, and Yao Wenyuan
3. The New Seekers; "True Love and Apple Pie"
4. Henry S. Ruth, Jr., and Charles Ruff
5. Elvis's funeral
6. Nixon's valet
7. Sadaharu Oh, the "Babe Ruth of Japan"
8. Werner Erhard's
9. House Speaker Carl Albert, who was next in line for the presidency from Agnew's resignation until Ford was confirmed as V.P., and after Ford became president until Rockefeller's confirmation
10. Ronald Biggs
11. The Jonestown mascot chimp. He was shot at the time of the mass suicides.
12. Two musk oxen; Milton and Matilda
13. General Duong Van Minh, who headed the government for two days—after President Thieu fled the country—before surrendering to the communists
14. Princess Leia, on the *Death Star* in *Star Wars*
15. "Way Back Home" by Junior Walker. They reportedly liked it because of the lines "Well, there's good and bad things about the South, boy/And some leave a bitter taste in my mouth/Like a black man livin' across the track/White man on the other side holdin' him back."

ABOUT THE AUTHORS

Marilyn Werden and David Arenson met in 1977 at the University of California, Santa Cruz. She was wearing a maxi skirt, and he had on a shirt with a collar as big as the wings of the space shuttle. They soon discovered a common fondness for cats, spicy food, and Godzilla movies—and the rest is history.

Despite newspaper careers in the 1980s, the couple, true to the spirit of the Me Decade, decided to chuck it all and do what felt right. They now live full-time in a recreational vehicle, traveling the country and writing.